George Washington and the
Immortal Moment
Yorktown, 1781

Published by Telford Publications*

Design by Andrew Evans Design
Cover illustration by David Eccles

© George T. Morrow II 2012

Telford Publications
301 Mill Stream Way,
Williamsburg, VA, U.S.A., 23185

Tel (757) 565-7215
Fax (757) 565-7216
www.williamsburgincharacter.com

FIRST EDITION

*Telford Publications is named for Alexander Telford,
a volunteer rifleman from Rockbridge County, Virginia, who
served in three Revolutionary War campaigns, in the last of which,
Yorktown, he was personally recognized by Gen. George Washington
for his extraordinary marksmanship with the long rifle.

Library of Congress Control Number: 2012932341
ISBN 978-0-9831468-5-8

Printed and bound by Sheridan Press, 450 Fame Avenue, Hanover, PA

George Washington
and the Immortal Moment
Yorktown, 1781

George T. Morrow II

WILLIAMSBURG IN CHARACTER

George Washington by Gilbert Stuart
"Portrait of a man who has become a face"

To Joan

"If a man could say nothing against a character but what he can prove, history could not be written."
SAMUEL JOHNSON

Contents

List of Illustrations

His Greatest Victory

Patcy, George Washington's 11-year-old stepdaughter, was plagued by agues or night sweats, the result of infection by malaria. There was no cure, though some doctors reported good results with a preparation made from the bark of the cinchona tree ("Peruvian Bark"). So it happened that when Washington went to Williamsburg in May of 1768 to attend the spring session of the House of Burgesses he brought Patcy along for a consultation with Dr. Arthur Lee, a 25-year-old graduate of the University of Edinburgh who had written his thesis on Peruvian Bark.[1] This was the same Dr. Lee who had just ended a two-year feud with local lawyer James Mercer; the same Dr. Lee who claimed to have detected a British plot against America. As James Mercer's father had recently put it, Lee's "scribblings" in the *Virginia Gazette* were killing his medical practice.[2] Yet here was Washington, bringing his "dear Patcy" to be seen by one of the most controversial men in Virginia.

Lee was so disliked that it is hard to know what Washington was thinking. There were other medical professionals he could have consulted, including Dr. John Sequeyra, reputedly the best doctor in Williamsburg, and Dr. William Pasteur, the city's leading apothecary.[3] Had Lee's diatribes struck a chord with Washington? Was there a political motive for his visit? We cannot be sure, but in taking Patcy to see Lee Washington was defying public opinion. His decision to entrust his stepdaughter to the care of a notorious rabble-rouser (albeit one from a good family) suggests the complex nature of the small world that was pre-Revolutionary Virginia. What it also suggests is the complexity of Washington himself: a quiet man with a placid demeanor, but one so fearful of committing the odd social gaffe that he had armored himself with 110 "Rules of Civility."[4]

As it happens, there was a sequel to this encounter, a return visit one month later to Mount Vernon by Arthur Lee and his brother William. "I never forgot," Lee wrote in 1777 of this visit, "your declaration when I had the pleasure of being at your House in 1768 that you was ready to take your Musket upon your Shoulder, whenever your Country call'd upon you. I heard that declaration with great satisfaction. I recollect it with the Same, & have seen it verify'd to your Immortal honor & the eminent advantage of the Illustrious cause in which we are contending." Washington noted the Lees' visit in his diary, but wrote nothing there about shouldering his musket. This was not surprising: as Washington once said, he used his dairy only to record "actions taken." Nor was it odd that Lee, who had hoped that his essays would inspire his countrymen to defend the "noble spirit of liberty" with their last breath, would recall Washington's declaration with satisfaction.[5]

Of the Revolution in Virginia, historian Edmund Randolph would later write, "Without an immediate oppression, without a cause depending so much on hasty feeling as theoretic reasoning, without a distaste for monarchy . . . the House of Burgesses in the year 1765 gave utterance to principles which within ten years were to expand into a revolution." Randolph's own candidate for prime mover of this revolution was, inevitably, Patrick Henry, Jr. More recently, Gordon Wood has enlarged on the idea of a rebellion without a cause, explaining that for all their talk of "British slavery" the Americans were not an oppressed people. "[T]hey had no crushing imperial shackles to throw off," writes Wood. "There was none of the legendary tyranny of history," "the American response was all out of proportion to the stimuli." Wood has yet to settle on a name for the leader of this disproportionate Revolution, suggesting only that the role seemed to call for a fiery personality with a heightened sense of grievance. With his reputation for stoical reserve, Washington would appear to be well out of the running. Yet, as the painter Gilbert Stuart once noted, the grim face staring down at us from his own and other portraits of Washington is less a model of inner calm than of calm brutally imposed, less an example of serenity than a monument to the high cost of repressing "ungovernable passions." "Had he lived among savage tribes [Stuart added] he would have been the fiercest of men."[6]

So whom are we to believe? Those who knew Washington or latter day myth-keepers seeking to make him a "late convert to active resistance" despite plain evidence to the contrary? For what had Washington done? He had made Arthur Lee, a volatile rabble-rouser, privy to sedition – this a bare three years after Patrick Henry had thought it politic to reply to a charge of treason by offering to shed his last drop of blood for George III. Apparently, Washington saw no reason to correct Lee's recollection of their dinner conversation. That could be because the issue was moot, the sedition of 1768 having become the war of 1777. Or, it might be because Washington and Lee were of like mind; that is, extremists in the cause of liberty.

Myths die hard; those attached to Founders die hardest of all. The iconic reserve of Washington seems as immutable as the marble from which it is often said to be fashioned. Joseph Ellis calls this the Mount Rushmore Washington – the founder myth at "its most virulent" – and suggests that we start our search for the inner man by knocking his statues off their pedestals.[7] Unhappily, this advice comes at a time when his name is still revered, but the man himself is all but unknown; when his face has become "iconic," but what it stands for is increasingly unclear.

Here was a man who set out to become great by portraying greatness in ever more difficult situations; who eventually became great, not only by great acts, but by great feats of self-mastery. He had a need for that self-mastery, too, in one well-known case making the leaves on the trees tremble at the violence of his oaths at the turncoat British Gen. Charles Lee. Yet another kind of self-mastery would be required in 1781, a year when he had to have men shot to save his army only to be saved in turn by a French-assisted victory over Gen. Cornwallis' at Yorktown. This book celebrates that victory and Washington's later apotheosis as the Father of His Country, but stops short of attributing the apotheosis to his deportment or the victory to his strategic vision. Military historians generally agree that the victory was inevitable once Cornwallis crawled into his "pudding bag"* at Yorktown, was sealed by Adm. de Grasse's victory over the British fleet at Cape Charles and solemnized in a surrender document that was, at best, anti-climactic.[8] It is the inner campaign that concerns us here: the providential victory of an emotionally-spent commander in chief who has begun to prepare his defense to an anticipated post-war board of inquiry; an apocryphal tribute from the beaten army to its conqueror for having "turned the world upside down." In the background is the wonder and awe of night time bombardments; a leader who sanctifies the earth under a tree just by sleeping there; followed by a rush of dramatic scenes and eerie coincidences, like the ones described on pages 42 to 51 and 73 to 78.

There are epochal moments in the history of a nation and the American victory at Yorktown is clearly one of them. It is

---

* The term comes from a comment by American Brig. Gen. George Weedon (1734–1793) at a staff meeting prior to the siege. Equipped with a draw string, the pudding bag is designed so that the pudding will retain its shape while it is being boiled.

the moment when a disorganized rabble became a nation; when a beloved leader became, in the words of King George III, "the greatest man in the world." But without an understanding of that great man's war with himself, his fierce unremitting struggle to control his emotions, neither the victory nor the man is intelligible. Properly read, the struggle reveals the man, a man capable of great mood swings as well as great powers of self-denial. As I believe that Washington's greatest victory was over himself, I have made his moods rather than his mode of prevailing at Yorktown my primary focus. The siege was relatively easy; the war within was more grueling. It would also last a lifetime.

George Washington and the Immortal Moment

Yorktown, 1781

"I will not repine – I have had my day."
George Washington, 8 Dec. 1784

The final portraits of George Washington are of a man who has become a face. With provocation – an overly familiar greeting was usually enough – the face became the man. "Oh, General!" cried the wife of the English Ambassador, Henrietta Liston, when she saw him at a levee in January of 1796, "your countenance shows your pleasure at the thought of retirement." "You are wrong," the President replied, "my countenance [has] never yet betrayed my feelings."[9]

If Washington in the final edition was bleak, the work in progress was truly grim. The war years were a time of demoralizing defeats and limited victories, of abject misery and superhuman endurance, of broken promises redeemed by mere chance and coincidence. Years of affecting the stoic had inured Washington to much of that pain, but not all of it – certainly not 1781, a year of abject misery capped by the quite unexpected gift of a victory at Yorktown, a victory so complete that when Lord North heard about it he cried, "Oh God! It is all over!"[10] That Washington should then simply retire from office and return to Mount Vernon was incredible to George III who told Benjamin West, "If he does that sir, he will be the greatest man in the world!"[11] What the King did not know was that the world's greatest man had been studying for that role all of his life.

The year 1781 began badly for Washington. In January, no less than half of the Pennsylvania Line revolted against the brutal discipline of their commanding officer, Gen. "Mad" Anthony Wayne. 1,250 soldiers and 67 artillerymen were discharged on their oath that they had been tricked by recruiters. Two of the leaders were shot. Wayne's division was then sent south to help Lafayette annoy Benedict Arnold in Virginia – though how an army of mutineers, four more of whom had to be shot en route, could be of much help was unclear. Then the New Jersey regiments revolted. Once again men were shot, this time on the orders of Washington himself who was now convinced that only "unconditional submission" could save the army.[12]

By January of 1781, the American commander in chief had reached his absolute nadir, "suspended in the Ball[anc]e, not from choice, but from hard and absolute necessity." The states were unable – or unwilling – to raise more than an eighth of their recruiting quotas. The army was "approaching fast to nakedness." The hospitals operated "without medicines." The decision to ask Louis XVI of France for a loan was quite literally an act of desperation. The letter Washington gave his emissary to the French king, Lt. Col. John Laurens, was blunt. The failure of the French fleet to support the campaign against Arnold, wrote Washington, was "much to be regretted . . . above all, because we stood in need of something, to keep us afloat." Realizing that this might sound too pessimistic, he put his reputation as "an honest and candid man . . . whose all depends on the final and happy termination of the present contest [behind the] . . . *opinion* that without a foreign loan our present force, (which is but the remnant of an army), cannot be kept together . . . . And if France delays . . . a timely, and powerful aid in the critical posture of our affairs it will avail us nothing should she attempt it hereafter . . . In a word . . . we are at the end of our tether, and . . . now or never our deliverance must come."[13]

France had been America's ally since 1778, yet it had done relatively little. This was not unintentional. The French wanted to be sure the revolution would succeed. They also had doubts about Washington himself. But for Lafayette's influence at court and the infatuation of the French public with Benjamin Franklin, they might have done nothing. And to be fair, when they did try – as in their recent attempt to retake Savannah – it was a disaster. Feelings of hopelessness and a sense of abandonment would be hard for anyone to overcome. For Washington, who took heart from the appearances of things, it was all but impossible.

It was "at this Epoch" (as Washington put it) that he did something very odd. Starting in May of 1781 he began to treat his diary as a vehicle for analysis and reflection. Until then, it had been a repository of names, dates and events or (as he put it) "actions taken." But there was something else that was odd about this diary. From the start, it was less about what was happening to him and his ragtag army than a *forecast* of "entries which may follow"; a list of "wants . . . and prospects" intended to be the sum of Washington's case detailing the perplexities of his personal situation while documenting "the embarrassed State" of his army. In short, this was not a diary at all. It was an "appeal to the facts," which is to say a quasi-legal defense of his conduct as commander in chief, not unlike the one he later advised Lafayette to make to "refute any charge." (Washington's only regret was that he had not done it "from the commencement of the War.") His diary from this period bears the mark of repeated revision. Yet, for the most part, the truth still shines through and what is lost in immediacy is more than made up for by a sense of impending doom.[14]

That Washington was now making a record of his desperation was not a good sign. In public, he continued to display determination. It was only in his diary that he envisioned disaster.

> Instead [he wrote in May] of having Magazines filled with provisions we have a scanty pittance scattered here & there . . . Instead of having our Arsenals well supplied with Military Stores, they are poorly provided, & the Workmen all leaving them. Instead of having the various articles of Field equipage in readiness to deliver, the Quarter Master General . . . is but now applying to the several States to provide these things . . . Instead of having a regular System of transportation established upon credit or funds in the Q[uarte]r Master's hands to defray the contingent expenses of it, we have neither . . . and all that business, or a great part of it, being done by Military Impress, we are daily & hourly oppressing the people – souring their tempers and alienating their affections. . . . scarce any State in the Union has . . . an eighth part of its quota [of men] in the field and little prospect . . . of ever getting more than half. In a word – instead of having everything in readiness to take the Field, we have nothing – and instead of having the prospect of a glorious offensive campaign before us, we have a bewildered, and gloomy defensive one – unless we should receive a powerful aid of Ships – Land Troops and Money from our generous allies.[15]

Everything depended on the French. Regrettably, "French promises [were] too contingent to build upon."[16] The phrase "French promises" embraced a lot, from the passionate optimism of Lafayette to the wintry politesse of the Comte de Rochambeau, the French commander in chief, whose

5,000-man army remained encamped at Newport, Rhode Island six months after its arrival in America. In fact, Rochambeau had good reason to remain aloof: "the country . . . in consternation" (his phrase), the American commander in chief – whom Rochambeau had met for the first time in Hartford a year ago, and whose proposal for a joint attack on the British stronghold in New York seemed to the Frenchman the foolish idea of a desperate man – ignorant of the most basic principles of war. New York was the headquarters of British forces in America; the home port of the British navy.[17]

No, the French army would stay right where it was. The French naval unit stationed at Newport required an army for its protection – which is to say, the ships were needed less to project French power than to provide an excuse for French inaction. And what of Washington's own army? Had the states met the recruiting quotas given to them by Congress? What about his supplies? Deftly, suavely, Rochambeau placed the onus back on Washington, showing him that his ability to command French forces in America stood, in Washington's words, "upon a very limited scale."[18] When he left Hartford, Washington was feeling as helpless as he had at any time during the war, while his French counterpart was more persuaded than ever that he was dealing with a novice. Nor was Rochambeau inclined to change his mind when Washington informed him on his return to New York that Maj. Gen. Benedict Arnold had gone over to the British – an act so unthinkable to Washington himself that when he heard the news he cried, "Arnold has betrayed us! Whom can we trust now?"[19]

It was more a *cri de coeur* than a question but one he was best advised to keep to himself. The elegant address and manners of the French commander in chief were enameled on iron. His closest aides spoke of being aggressively quizzed in "disagreeable and . . . insulting" ways. Otherwise, as French Chief

Commissary Claude Blanchard said, Rochambeau was inclined to affect the haughty French nobleman and professional soldier surrounded by "rascals or idiots."[20] Had the frigate *Concorde* not arrived at Boston on May 8 with new orders from Louis XVI, it is not clear that Rochambeau would ever have ventured his army in what looked, increasingly, like a lost cause. Happily, the dispatches borne by his son, the Vicomte de Rochambeau, were clear: The first ordered the French commander to promptly commit his army to the offensive. The second told him of the King's decision to donate 6,000,000 livres to the American cause. Yet another informed him that Adm. de Grasse had set sail for the West Indies on March 22 with 26 French ships of the line, 8 frigates and 150 transports with 4,000 troops, 3,000 of them marines. At least some of this news was shared with Washington who promptly asked for a council of war. Rochambeau consented and on May 21–22 the two generals and their staffs gathered at Wethersfield, Connecticut.

What Washington wanted from this meeting was a plan of attack for New York. What Rochambeau wanted is less clear, though he tried to project a spirit of amity and cooperation. Washington would leave Wethersfield convinced that there had been a complete meeting of minds. Had his campaign plan not been put in writing and signed by everyone present at the conference? Still, perhaps it would not be a bad idea – with history looking on – to record the terms of the agreement in his diary: "Fixed with Count de Rochambeau upon a plan of Campaign – in Substance as follows. That the French Land force (except 200 Men) should March so soon as the Squadron [the French fleet at Newport] could Sail for Boston – to the

The Count de Rochambeau "Surrounded by rascals and idiots"

North River & there, in conjunction with the American [army] ... commence an operation against New York ... or to extend our views to the Southward as circumstances and a Naval superiority might render more necessary & eligible."[21] The reason for preferring New York, Washington wrote, was the "reduced state" of the British garrison there and attrition to his own army were it to be marched through Virginia in the sweltering summer heat.[22]

The meeting over, Rochambeau and his staff set out on their return to Newport. Washington stayed on in Wethersfield, according to his diary, to draft and forward dispatches. The Governors of four New England states were asked in the most "earnest and pointed terms, to complete their Continental Battalions for the Campaign, at least, if it could not be done for the War or 3 Years – to hold a body of Militia ready to March in one Week after being called for."[23] Massachusetts and Connecticut were specifically told of the army's need for "Powder and the means of Transport." It was sunset on the 25th of May by the time Washington returned to his camp at New Windsor, New York. Nine days later, French cavalry leader and Brig. Gen. Lauzun rode in with an urgent dispatch from Rochambeau.

We have Lauzun's word for it that Washington raged for days over that dispatch. It seemed that a second French council of war had set aside his plan of attack immediately after he left. There would be no joint assault on New York; the fleet would stay where it was, at least for now. This was dismaying news, delaying, if not obviating, any hope of a "glorious offensive campaign." The elaborate courtesies invoked by Washington in his reply, offering to support the fleet's removal to New York, were, if nothing else, a sign that he was feeling anything but polite.

I must adhere to my former opinion and to the plan which was fixed at Wethersfield as most eligible ... I would not however set up my single judgment against that of so many Gentlemen of experience, more especially as the matter partly depends upon a knowledge of Marine Affairs of which I candidly express my ignorance.[24]

He was much less guarded in a letter to Gen. Rochambeau's aide, the Marquis de Chastellux.[25] He then sent a letter to Lafayette detailing the Wethersfield accord as if it were still in effect, adding that a Virginia campaign had been ruled out "as we had not command of the water."[26] The letter was intercepted by the British and seized upon by the British commander in chief, Sir Henry Clinton, as conclusive proof that the allies had now shifted their focus to New York. Immediately, Cornwallis was ordered to go to the Virginia Peninsula to await transport to New York. The fatal error that was to lead to the defeat of British arms in America was duly celebrated by Rochambeau in a post war memoir but only by way of censuring Washington's indiscretion – a view vigorously opposed by James Thomas Flexner in his four volume life of Washington. In Flexner's view, the intercepted letter was deliberately leaked by Washington, because he wanted to "take pressure off the south by frightening Clinton," an analysis which seeks to make Washington a prophet to qualify him as a military genius but which fails to allow for the genuine desperation of a man in need of something – anything – to keep his spirits up.[27] In any case, from this time forward Clinton was convinced that the allies' real objective was New York.[28]

After the war, Washington would seek to adjust the record to reflect the result, reworking the disorderly landscape of war until his escape from disaster seemed predestined – which is to say, he revised his diary. But he could not revise his letter to the King of France. His plea for money and guns to Louis XVI did not say that his army was "at the end of *its* tether." It said "*we* are at the end of *our* tether." It did not just ask for help; it asked for "deliverance," a word that, figuratively at least, took him beyond a call for help to a plea for heavenly intervention. That Washington was seeking help from the ruler (by divine right) of Europe's most repressive regime might be amusing were it not so clearly a function of his growing conviction that the war was lost. Similarly, his May 31 letter to the Marquis de Lafayette might have been merely indiscreet, the desperate act of a man hoping against hope, or a canny ruse to throw the British off the scent. If the letter was a ruse, it was certainly a paradoxical one, as Washington continued, in his dispatches to the French and in his diary, to press the case for New York.[29] Of course, if the war was lost, his country would expect him to revert to the *character Washington*, preserving the face that had "never yet betrayed his feelings." No, he would not give up; he would emulate the stoic Cato. But he might, just for a moment, think about how this would all look to future historians.

There was another reason Washington was dwelling on his "expiring hopes": his growing conviction that he was a minor character in a drama orchestrated by others.[30] It was more of a feeling than a fact, and Washington was hardly one to document his sense of helplessness. The fact is, however, that when Rochambeau finally summoned de Grasse and his fleet to the Chesapeake, he did so by secret courier and without informing the American commander in chief. Upon reaching Virginia, the French admiral was directed to send a dispatch to Rochambeau, who then "*might* take the earliest opportunity to combine our march with that of General Washington so as to proceed by land as expeditiously as possible and join him at any . . . part of the Chesapeake." (A seaport, such as Portsmouth, Virginia, would do very nicely.)[31] Not until the 14th of August was Washington given any precise information on the whereabouts of de Grasse.

The truth is, Washington owed his victory at Yorktown entirely to the French. He could see (after the fact) that de Grasse's appearance in the Chesapeake was no accident. That the French fleet was summoned to forestall his foolhardy New York plan was harder to accept. One thing Washington could not have missed was Gen. Rochambeau's contempt for himself. A French officer who was present at Wethersfield said Rochambeau used Washington with "all the ungraciousness and all the unpleasantness possible," with the result that Washington left the council of war (according to this officer) "with a sad and disagreeable feeling in his heart."[32] As the commander in chief of a naked army, embarrassed by traitors and mutineers alike, Washington would seem to be a particularly good candidate for a sad and disagreeable feeling. But it seems there was more to this meeting with Rochambeau and his staff than French rudeness. In a 1779 letter, Washington had told Lafayette that he found talking "through the medium of an interpreter . . . so extremely awkward, insipid, and [so] uncouth that I could scarce bear it in idea" (He was speaking of the humiliation of not being able to speak French "with [French] *Ladies.*")[33] That a man so jealous of his dignity could not bear a social disability is hardly surprising. If knowledge of French was not the parole of learned men, it was at least the mark of a gentleman. But how much worse to appear uncouth in a war council with the proud Comte de Rochambeau! If Washington seemed sad, ill at ease – even foolish – at Wethersfield, it may be because that was how he felt.

In the end, each man was to discover that he had greatly underestimated the other. Over the next thirty days, despite being constantly assailed by fresh surprises and reverses – so many they would have driven a weaker man to distraction – Washington managed to endure, while Rochambeau went from contempt to grudging respect, to something like affection for his American counterpart. Meanwhile, Washington was receiving frequent solicitations from the governors of the States, Thomas Jefferson among them, pressing him to drop everything and "repair thither" at once. The situation in the States was portrayed to him as virtually hopeless and in some cases it was. But it is also true that more than a few of these appeals were inflated to avert blame for what some governors privately believed was an impending disaster. On June 13 Washington received a dispatch from Rochambeau enclosing a letter from de Grasse saying that he was bringing his fleet to the coast of North America around the 15th of July. The next day, he received the agreeable news that Gen. Nathaniel Greene had retaken Charleston. Two days later, Washington detached some of his "weakliest Men" to re-garrison West Point, the post Arnold had intended to betray in return for a general's commission in the British army. On the 24th Washington got a letter from Rochambeau saying he was marching for New York. The next day, his wife, Martha, who had been with him since November 1780, left for Virginia so "extremely unwell with a kind of Jaundice" (Washington's words) that he now feared for her life. Finally, on the 29th, he got a letter from Lafayette informing him of the near seizure of the Virginia Assembly by British dragoons. (The delegates had managed to escape to a nearby inn but at such cost to their dignity that the proprietress refused to believe that Patrick Henry could be among them.)[34]

A week later the two allied armies effected a junction at White Plains, New York. For Washington, this was an opportunity to appear as the leader of a grand army of 10,000 men, a chance to strike a martial pose, for his own sake and for his beleaguered army. The French had just finished a long and grueling march over dusty roads. But they put on clean uniforms, stuck feathers in their hats and, trailed by a marching band, filed off smartly in front of an array of local ladies and gentlemen. This elegant exhibition by one of Europe's best-dressed armies operated like a tonic on everyone. For Washington, who was never greater than when portraying greatness, it was almost a rebirth. A French officer (and a sympathetic one at that) described the army facing him across the green as an epitome of hardship and want, with the notable exception of the mostly black 1st Rhode Island Regiment:

> In beholding this army I was struck, not by its smart appearance, but by its destitution: the men were without uniforms and covered with rags; most of them were barefoot. They were of all sizes, down to children who could not have been over fourteen. There were many Negroes, mulattoes, etc. Only their artillerymen were wearing uniforms. These are the elite of the country and are actually very good troops, well schooled in their profession. We had nothing but praise for them later; their officers who seemed to have good practical training, were the only ones with whom we occasionally lived. I returned, following the generals of the French army, who looked quite different and much more glamorous.[35]

A soldier of the 1st Rhode Island Regiment "The élite of the country"

If the French believed that mere boys could be good soldiers, well-schooled in the manual of arms, it was because they were professionals and, well, France expected them to do their duty. If Washington believed it, it was because, for the first time in the war, he was looking beyond barefoot boys to a brilliant array of French general officers prepared to call him commander in chief.

Afterwards, Rochambeau asked Washington for his "definitive plan" of attack for New York to give to de Grasse – an attack, based on his letter to de Grasse, that he had little intention of mounting. Be that as it may, Washington should not have been surprised by this request. It was no more than a list of the particulars needed to give effect to the Wethersfield agreement. Particulars were critical. De Grasse was about to begin a series of orchestrated movements that would bring him to the point of attack. At the very least he needed to know where he was going. Regrettably, the American commander did not have such a plan. Worse, he seemed to lack the ability to come up with one. In a diary entry notable for its stammering syntax, Washington tried to explain:

> Count de Rochambeau having called upon me, in the name of Count de Barras, for a definitive plan of Campaign, that he might communicate it to the Count de Grasse – I could not but acknowledge, that the uncertainties under which we labour – the few Men who have joined (either as Recruits for the Continental Battns or Militia) & the ignorance in which I am kept by some of the States on whom I mostly depended – especially Massachusetts [from] whose Govr. I have not received a line since I addressed him from Weathersfd. the 23rd of May last – rendered it impracticable for me to do more than to prepare, first, for the enterprise against New York as agreed to at Weathersfield and secondly for the relief of the Southern States if after all my efforts, & earnest application to these States it should be found at the arrivl. of Count de Grasse that I had neither Men, nor means adequate to the first object.[36]

Those who have seen Washington's letters to Sally Fairfax* and his September 2, 1781 letter to Lafayette will be familiar with the style of this entry. Contrary to myth, he did not repress powerful emotion; he enacted it, in his letters and diaries, throwing off dashes like sparks, interrupting himself

* See The Man Behind the Face, p.59

with interjections, only then to lurch off in a new direction. Were it not for the final intervention of a period, the paragraph above might have wandered into chaos or, unthinkable for Washington, self-pitying recrimination.

There were reasons why Washington was unable to produce a plan of attack for New York. But first there was the need to justify himself, to lay additional groundwork for his post-war defense.[37] The governors of the States had ignored his "earnest applications"; he had "neither Men, nor means." But this was not the main reason; the main reason was that Washington was out of his depth. Despite his grand title, he was no commander in chief, nor was he a practitioner of the art of war. More to the immediate point, he knew nothing of sieges, a skill in which the French were said to be masters. Finally, if Washington's *viva voce* response to Rochambeau's request was anything like his diary entry for that date it must have done little to change the French commander's view that he was dealing with a fool.

Washington was not a defeated man. But he had lived too long with the idea of defeat. Never a great military mind, he was now at risk of losing his character as well as the war. Later, he may have wondered why Rochambeau had asked him for a plan he never intended to use. The answer was that because from the day he arrived in America, Rochambeau had been the recipient of annoying demands from Lafayette that he put aside caution and orders for Washington's sake; because Rochambeau's son had told him that the same French officers who lavished praise on the "majestic" Washington in their letters home never failed to disparage their own less charismatic leader; because, despite his enemies at court, he would by now have become French Secretary of War had he not been in America, dealing (as he said) "with scanty resources and distressing predicaments."[38] Here was a chance to teach his ally a lesson in humility and finally call the question on New York. The disarray in Washington's diary for the date suggests Rochambeau succeeded on both counts. But Washington seems to have also passed the one test that mattered to Rochambeau: the test of honesty.

Meanwhile, Washington was doing his best to entertain his allies in proper style. This was no small task in an army unable to feed itself. But somehow Washington managed to serve dinner to thirty officers of the French general staff every day for a month. This did not stop them from carping about his weak coffee and overly-acidic salad dressing. On the other hand, the French were enormously impressed by the easy informality of the dinners, how long the Americans sat at table and the "free, agreeable" (and ribald) nature of their toasts.[39] Ever careful of his dignity, Washington drank little, content to smile and crack the odd hickory nut while he listened. It was not long before he and his ragtag army began to acquire a certain dignity. Baron von Closen was amazed that "soldiers composed of men of every age, even of children of fifteen, of whites and blacks, almost naked, unpaid and rather poorly fed, can march so well and stand fire so steadfastly." This he ascribed to Washington's "calm and calculated measures" – measures which von Closen seemed to think qualified Washington as a truly great commander in chief. "[D]aily [I] discover some new and eminent qualities [in him]," von Closen continued, "He is certainly admirable as the leader of his army, in which everyone regards him as his father and friend."[40]

On July 22 Rochambeau and Washington rode out to survey New York's defenses. Here was another chance to strike a pose, and Washington took full advantage of it. Seven days later, he received a letter from Adm. de Barras, commander of the French fleet in Newport, referring him to his earlier letter to Rochambeau in cypher, stating "in stronger terms than heretofore his disinclination to [sail from] Newport till the arrival of Adm[ira]l de Grasse." "This induced me [continued Washington] to desist from further representing the advantages . . . [of] preventing a junction of the enemy's forces at New York." Had he now given up on New York? It certainly *seemed* that he had. Despite the fact that his army was "in perfect readiness" for the attack on New York, he was willing to "seriously [consider] . . . an operation to the Southward." Was he conceding that his New York plan made no sense or simply conceding that he was an actor in a drama orchestrated by others? It seemed the latter: he was concerned that "the loss of or damage to" the French fleet would be "ascribed to [his] obstinacy in urging a measure to which [Rochambeau's] judgment was oppos'd."[41]

The good news of the "departure of the Count de Grasse from [the West Indies] . . . with between 25 & 29 Sail of the line & 3200 land Troops on the 3[rd of August]" was duly noted by Washington in his diary for August 14, but now it framed prospects for Virginia. There would be no more aimless maneuvering. Rather, everything was to be put "in the most perfect readiness to commence . . . operations in the moment of [de Grasse's] arrival . . . in the West Indies by the Middle of October." Washington explained, "Matters having now come to a crisis and a decisive plan to be determined on, I was obliged . . . to give up all idea of attacking New York; and instead . . . remove the French Troops and a detachment from the American Army to the Head of Elk [the head of Chesapeake Bay] to be transported to Virginia for the purpose of co-operating with the force from the West Indies against the Troops in that State." There it was: capitulation on New York in return for a new sense of urgency and a new plan of action. This was no small thing after months of hollow French promises and querulous letters from the governors of the States. He was still anxious, but for now anxiety had to compete with a previously unforeseen hope of a war-ending victory.[42]

The next day, Washington dispatched a rider to Virginia to order the Marquis de Lafayette to block Cornwallis' path to North Carolina. On 16 August he received a letter from Lafayette telling him that Cornwallis had landed at Yorktown and was seen "throwing up Works." At once, the pace of Washington's diary quickened: subsequently, his orders would be issued in the first person, the voice of the commander in chief reasserting itself in keeping with the greatness of the opportunity. An entry about "a slow and disagreeable March" became a bracing exercise in *self*-command; its dash-filled sequel, a portrayal of the warrior mentality, with clauses dispatched like couriers. The New York plan was revived, but now it was a feint for an attack on Cornwallis in Virginia. The New Jersey troops he had left overlooking British defenses in New York as a precaution were ordered to "create apprehensions" among the British that he was headed for Staten Island. Meanwhile, Quartermaster Gen. Benjamin Lincoln was directed to speed the "transportation of the [American] Troops across the [Hudson] River." Within days, the entire American army and all of its supplies had crossed over to New Jersey. Another march south, Washington wrote, and the "real object [would be revealed] to the enemy."[43] But where was de Grasse? No one seemed to know. While he awaited more news, Washington split his army into three columns and sent them to Sandy Hook, New Jersey, a good place to meet de Grasse if New York were still the objective, but also an excellent jumping-off place for Virginia. It was a prudent move; but for Washington, yet another vexing, shying-away from "precious opportunity."[44]

The army's most pressing need, Washington told his diary, was troop transports.[45] The boats arrived, only to be found inadequate, whereupon Washington ordered the van of the army to march to the Head of Elk, the next place of embarkation for Virginia. There being still no news of de Grasse, he then joined Rochambeau and Philadelphia financier Robert Morris for a grand dinner and toasts to His Most Christian Majesty, Louis XVI. The next day, Washington conducted another ego-satisfying review of the two armies on parade – followed by a salute from Rochambeau, standing (with hat doffed in respect) *en suite* with his generals and the members of Congress on the steps of Philadelphia's Independence Hall. In ways great and small, the American leader was being pushed forward by his countrymen and the French (neither of whom could now afford to do without him) and caused to be the great man he seemed.[46]

Bracing though this was, it could do little to relieve a man ailing from *too much* hope. What followed, a sudden overflow of powerful emotion to the one man capable of returning it with interest, Lafayette, is one of the most unguarded letters he ever wrote:

> But my dear Marquis I am distressed beyond expression, to know what is become of the Comte de Grasse, and for fear the English Fleet, by occupying the Chesapeake (towards which my last accounts say they were steering) should frustrate all our flattering prospects in that quarter. I am also not a little solicitous for the Count de Barras, who was to have sailed from Rhode Island on the 23d . . . and from whom I have heard nothing since that time. Of many contingencies we will hope for the most propitious events.
>
> Should the retreat of Lord Cornwallis by water be cut off by the arrival of either of the French Fleets, I am persuaded you will do all in your power to prevent his escape

by land. May that great felicity be reserved for you!

You see how critically important the present Moment is: for my own part I am determined to persist, with unremitting ardour in my present Plan, unless some inevitable and insuperable obstacles are thrown in our way.

Adieu, my Dear Marquis! If you get any thing New from any quarter, send it I pray you, *on the Spur of Speed*, for I am almost all impatience and anxiety. (Italics in original.) 47

It was the letter of a man steeled for failure, and all but unmanned by the prospect of success. There were no genteel, 18th Century civilities to convey such feelings. There were only the feelings themselves, rendered in tremulous italics, as if groaning under the weight of "distress . . . beyond expression."

On September 5th, the rear echelon of the French army reached Philadelphia. By now, even Sir Henry Clinton could see that the allied army was moving to the southward.48 Meanwhile, Washington had gone to the Head of Elk to hasten the embarkation. En route, in the town of Chester, he received the "agreeable news" of de Grasse's arrival in Chesapeake Bay "with 28 Sail of the line and four frigates [carrying] . . . 3000 land Troops."49 Unlike spur of speed, the phrase that had launched his newfound optimism, "agreeable news" got no extra emphasis. Nor was it needed: with victory now a real possibility, Washington retook command of himself. Anticipating the style of his postwar revisions, his diary reverted to a more normal word order. The dashes of a man afflicted with too much hope

"Even Sir Henry Clinton could see that the Allied army was moving to the southward"

yielded to the uninflected prose of the commander in chief. To be sure, this was meant to be "a concise Journal of Military transactions," not a confessional. There were also the appearances to be thought of: achieving a dignity in words equal to the occasion. But for attentive observers, it was not the anxiety of hope that he was writing out of his life, it was spontaneity.

Even in Washington's own day, this would have seemed rather odd. We can say that because we know, based upon eyewitness accounts, that his initial reaction to the news of de Grasse's arrival was very different from that described in his much-revised diary. As the Comte de Deux Ponts later recalled it, Washington's "natural coldness" dissolved at once.[50] He was a "child whose every wish had been gratified" – or, as the Comte de Dumas put it, "I have never seen a man more overcome with great and sincere joy than was General Washington."[51] Granting the exhilarating nature of the news and a certain largesse in French accounts of the majestic Washington, this was, at least, a remarkable transformation. But there was more to come. When he finished reading the dispatch, Washington rode off to Chester, intending to deliver the news to Rochambeau himself. He was there, at the end of Chester wharf, jumping up and down, "waving his hat and white handkerchief joyfully" as Rochambeau's boat slowly came into view. Like Deux Ponts, Baron von Closen was so stunned by the sight of the six-foot-three Washington jumping up and down for joy that he was rendered nearly speechless: "One must experience such circumstances [he explained] to appreciate the effect that such gratifying news can have, particularly upon young people who are burning with the desire to try their strength against the enemy and avid for glory, as we all were." But an even greater marvel was to follow: "Rochambeau and Washington embraced *warmly* on the shore." (Emphasis in the original.)

The bonhomie, the conviction that victory was inevitable

now spread to the entire army. Dr. James Thacher, a surgeon with the Pennsylvania Regiments, described the mood this way: "Our situation reminds me of some theatrical exhibition, where the interest and expectations of the spectators are continually increasing, and where curiosity is wrought to the highest point. Our destination has for some time [been a] matter of perplexing doubt and uncertainty; bets have run high for some time that we were to occupy the ground marked out on the Jersey shore, to aid in the siege of New York, and on the other, that we are stealing a march on the enemy and are actually destined to Virginia in pursuit of the army under Lord Cornwallis."[52] On August 21, with its destination no longer a secret, the army entered Philadelphia. Thacher's account captures the prevailing mood, a mood more in accord with a Roman triumph:

The streets [of Philadelphia, wrote Thacher] being extremely dirty, and the weather warm and dry, we raised a dust like a smothering snowstorm, blinding our eyes and covering our bodies with it; this was not a little mortifying, as the ladies were viewing us from the open windows of every house as we passed . . . Our line of march, including appendages and attendants, extended nearly two miles. The general officers and their aids, in rich military uniforms, mounted on noble steeds elegantly caparisoned, were followed by their servants and baggage. In the rear of every brigade were several field-pieces, accompanied by ammunition carriages. The soldiers marched in slow and solemn step, regulated by the drum and fife. In the rear followed a great number of wagons, loaded with tents, provisions and other baggage, such as a few soldiers' wives and children; though a very small number of these are allowed to encumber us on this occasion.[53]

Thacher's image of a snowstorm of dust was no less vivid for
being the result of bad dirt roads, a torrid summer day and a
tired, shuffling army. Nor was his description any less striking
for its reliance on clichés like "noble steeds elegantly
caparisoned" and funereal-sounding "slow and solemn" steps.
For Thacher, for many Americans, the greatness of the occasion required the greatest of metaphors and, while the *mot juste*
may have eluded them, their reach for it fairly described the
arc of their rapture: Philadelphia retaken! The French in white
uniforms! A grand marching band! As Thacher neatly put it,
the French marching band operated on everyone "like
enchantment."[54] From now on, every diary entry – every letter
written by an American – seemed fraught with awe. Much of
this awe was directed at the American commander in chief who
could be relied on to bear it well. But "feu de joies," the
impromptu celebratory salutes of foot soldiers' muskets, were
the army's awe, the most recent of which marked a conver-
gence: the 4th of July and Cornwallis' withdrawal to Yorktown.

For once, Washington's Orders for the day expressed unbri-
dled optimism: "As no circumstance could possibly have
happened more opportunely in point of time, no prospect
could ever have promised more important successes, and nothing but our want of exertions can probably blast the pleasing
prospects before us."[55] "From then on," wrote the Baron von
Closen, "the soldiers . . . spoke of Cornwallis as if they had
already captured him."[56] Victory, so recently a forlorn hope,
was that certain. But for the "naturally cold" Washington, the
anxiety of too much hope now had to compete with the anxiety borne of too little information.

The anxiety was real enough: without the pursuing menace
of Rochambeau's professionals and the French fleet to box him
in, Cornwallis might yet escape his pudding bag at Yorktown.
But if Washington left Chester as anxious as he came, he was

not so anxious as to fail to order Gen. Benjamin Lincoln to load the transports and send the rest of the army marching south. With that, he, Rochambeau and their aides galloped off to Virginia, but at such a pace that by the time Washington reached Baltimore, he had left the entire general staff of both armies in his dust. Only his slave manservant Will Lee was with him when he arrived at Mount Vernon on the 9th of September. Washington had not been there for six years. Four months ago, with the cause apparently lost, he must have thought he would never see it again. Now he was on the verge of winning the war. His aide (and later portraitist), Jonathan Trumbull, sketched in words the dinner that Washington laid on at Mount Vernon that evening for a party of 70 American and French officers: "A numerous family now present. All accommodated. An elegant seat and situation great appearance of opulence and real exhibitions of hospitality and princely entertainment."[57]

On September 12, the two generals and their staff officers left for Williamsburg. Washington's dispatch to Gen. Lincoln enjoined him to hurry his men "on the wing of Speed,"[58] while a p.s. to Lafayette teasingly hoped he would " keep Cornwallis safe . . . until we arrive."[59] Only twenty miles down the road, he was halted by the now ten day-old news that de Grasse was engaged with a large English fleet. Unfortunately, the rider had left before the outcome was clear! Washington was again free to think the worst. At once, he despatched a rider with an order directing Gen. Lincoln to stop the transports and put the men ashore at Head of Elk. He and Rochambeau then rode on, but at such a reckless pace that only two weary aides (out of the original 70) were still at their sides when they reached Williamsburg.[60]

The two generals entered the city without fanfare, riding past Lafayette's camp at the rear of the College so quickly that

the soldiers there were unable to do them the usual military
honors:

> [T]he French line had just time to form. [St. George
> Tucker recalled] The Continentals had more leisure.
> [Gen. Washington] approached without any pomp or
> parade, attended only by a few horsemen and his own ser-
> vants. The Comte de Rochambeau and Gen. Hand, with
> one or two more officers, were with him. I met him as I
> was endeavoring to get to camp from town in order to
> parade the brigade; but he had already passed it. To my
> great surprise he recognized my features and spoke to me
> immediately after. Never was more joy painted in any
> countenances than theirs. The Marquis rode up with pre-
> cipitation, clasped the General in his arms and embraced
> him with an ardor not easily described.[61]

Later, St. George Tucker elaborated on that not-to-be described
ardor: "at this moment, we saw the Marquis, riding in at full
speed from the town, and as he approached General Washington, threw his bridle on the horse's neck, opened both his arms
as wide as he could reach, and caught the General round his
body, hugged him as close as it was possible, and absolutely
kissed him from ear to ear once or twice."[62] Despite the undig-
nified nature of his young friend's enthusiasm, Washington
seemed to bear it well: his face was said to be "painted" with joy
– a reaction very different from his response in 1796 when, to
win a bet, his old friend Gouveneur Morris placed a hand on
Washington's shoulder and declared, "My dear General, how
happy I am to see you look so well.'" [63] This indecent familiar-
ity elicited the predictable reaction. Washington removed the
offending hand, stepped back and glared. (We are told that
Morris shrank away in the crowd.)

"The whole army [continued Tucker] and all the town were

presently in motion. The General – at the request of the Marquis de St. Simon – rode through the French lines, then visited the Continental line. As he entered the camp the cannon from the park of artillery and from every brigade announced the happy event. His train by this time was much increased; and men, women and children seemed to vie with each other in demonstrations of joy and eagerness to see their beloved countryman."[64] Washington lodged in the George Wythe house; Rochambeau at the home of Speaker Peyton Randolph, the deceased first President of the Continental Congress. That evening, the Marquis de St. Simon entertained Washington and the officers of both armies: "To add to the happiness of the evening [said an observer] an elegant band of music [the French marching band] played an introductive part of a French opera, signifying the happiness of the family when blessed with the presence of their father, and their great dependence upon him. About ten o'clock the company rose up, and after mutual congratulations and the greatest expressions of joy, they separated."[65] "We are all alive and so sanguine in our hopes [wrote St. George Tucker] that nothing can be conceived more different than the countenances of the same men at this time and on the first of June. . . . Cornwallis may now tremble for his fate, for nothing but some extraordinary interposition of his guardian angel seems capable of saving him and his whole army."[66]

On September 14 Washington learned the results of the battle of Cape Charles: In a three hour battle, de Grasse (with help from Adm. de Barras) had captured three British ships, the frigates *Iris* and *Richmond* and the 44-gun *Romulus*, which were being sent to Head of Elk to help bring down troops and the apparatus for a siege.[67] If this was not a great victory, it had at least made one possible. Adm. Graves was on his way back to New York.

That afternoon, the officers of both armies paid their respects to the American commander in chief, who stood in the doorway of the George Wythe house and took each man by the hand. In all directions, said one American officer, troops could be seen exercising under the direction of "their great military oracle," the so-called "Drillmaster of the Revolution," Baron von Steuben, who could "always be found waiting with one or two aides on horseback." Under his stern eye, the men went through their evolutions in front of "many officers and spectators," after which the entire unit "march[ed] off, saluting the Baron and field officers of the day, as they pass[ed]."[68]

On the 17th, de Grasse sent the *Queen Charlotte*, a captured officers' launch, up the James to bring Washington and Rochambeau to a meeting aboard his flagship, the *Ville de Paris*. Having borne Rochambeau's contempt and Lafayette's ardor, Washington was more prepared than he otherwise might have been for

The George Wythe House
"Washington took each officer by the hand"

de Grasse's greeting when he stepped aboard the *Ville de Paris*. "My dear little General!" cried six-foot-four de Grasse, to the six-foot-three Washington.[69] We are told that Washington also had to submit to another French kiss. He could well afford it. De Grasse told him what he had come to hear: that he would remain off Hampton for two weeks. With business out of the way, Washington and Rochambeau then joined de Grasse and his officers for an elegant dinner aboard the *Ville de Paris*. Around ten p.m., the two generals and their party returned to the *Queen Charlotte* for the trip back up the James. Unfortunately, the wind had shifted: it was now blowing from the west, downriver and away from Williamsburg. Not until four days later were Washington and Rochambeau able to get back to Williamsburg. This maddening delay was succeeded by an even more maddening letter from de Grasse.

It seemed that the French fleet had to return at once to the West Indies. This was not entirely a surprise. De Grasse had said from the start that he would have to go back to the Caribbean in October to refit. But to leave now, on the very eve of a battle that could end the war! Washington's dictated reply lacked the dashes of his note to Lafayette, but not for a sense of urgency. Anger, barely sublimated in a list of likely bad consequences, tumbled out of his letter. The fleet's departure, Washington said, would create "an opening for the succour of York[town] which the enemy wd instantly avail himself of, would frustrate these brilliant prospects, and the consequences would be not only the disgrace and loss of renouncing [the] . . . enterprise . . . but the disbanding . . . [of] the whole Army."[70] He could not conceal the painful anxiety he had been under "since the receipt of [de Grasse's] letter." Finally, de Grasse was told that he would be blamed for the result: "if you sh[ou]ld withdraw . . . no future day can restore us a similar occasion for striking a decisive blow. . . even a momentary absence of the French fleet may expose us to loss of the British."[71]

Unable to plead his case in French, Washington asked Lafayette to deliver the letter. But to Lafayette's surprise, when he met with de Grasse he found the French admiral had as little interest in discussing Washington's letter as he did in leaving Virginia. Instead, they talked about biscuits, beds and British spies. It seemed that de Grasse had changed his mind.[72] Lafayette wrote to Washington to say that he *supposed* de Grasse would now stay. Washington supposed that he would too. Victory – so inconceivable a bare month ago – was now, suddenly, at hand.

The two armies left Williamsburg on September 28, the

Americans in front, Gen. de Saint-Simon's three regiments in the center and Rochambeau's contingent in the rear. When they were within four miles of Yorktown, they split into three ranks and enveloped the city. "The heat that day [the Comte de Clermont-Crevecoeur later recalled] was incomparably worse than anything we had previously endured. . . . I was on foot, since my horses had not yet arrived, a plight I shared with all the other officers in the army. Even the generals were not all mounted. I can testify to having suffered every affliction imaginable. We left nearly 800 soldiers in the rear. Two fell at my feet and died on the spot."[73] For Pvt. Joseph P. Martin it was simply "a warm day." Unlike the rigidly-disciplined French, Martin's Pennsylvanians were permitted to stop and cook a meal. They were also allowed to take off their coats and unbutton their waistcoats.[74] The way the two armies dealt with the Virginia heat was a token of deeper differences. The Americans, who preferred to run away to fight another day, took a casual view of their dress. The French, in wool uniforms designed for a European climate, never did adapt to warfare in America.

Happily, Britain's tactical mistakes trumped France's sartorial inflexibility. "The roads the enemy should have defended foot by foot were clear," noted Gen. Clermont-Crevecoeur. "We were never molested in any way, though we had expected to be."[75] There was a brief display of annoyance from the British cavalry when the Americans reached Yorktown, but it ended quickly (according to Trumbull) "upon our bringing up some field pieces and making a few shot, they retire, and we take a quiet position for the night." Washington and his aides slept on bare ground covered by the boughs of an ancient oak, which, Trumbull predicted, would now "probably be rendered venerable . . . for time to come."[76]

The next day, the three armies took their places for the

denouement. Cornwallis, behind a ring of earthen redoubts fronting on Yorktown, had his back to the river. The French army was on his right, the Americans on his left and the allied artillery in the center. On the 30th, much to Washington's delight, the British general abandoned his outer defenses. "We immediately take possession [wrote Trumbull] . . . of the . . . redoubts, and find ourselves unexpectedly upon very advantageous ground, commanding their works in near approach."[77] The British guns were now firing incessantly, though with little effect. The French and American cannons and seige guns – there were now more than 120 – had yet to fire a single shot. Meanwhile, French and American sappers were digging parallels to the British lines, erecting gabions and fosses in the European style of siege warfare of which the French were the acknowledged masters.

In the American lines, a few soldiers exhibited a bravado that defies belief. James Duncan described a Virginia militiaman, "possessed of more bravery [than] prudence, [who] stood constantly on the parapet and d[amne]d his soul 'if he would dodge for the buggers.'" He escaped longer than might have been expected, brandishing a spade at every ball that was fired his way, until one came and put an end to his capers. Duncan was no less disgusted with his own, otherwise esteemed commanding officer, Col. Alexander Hamilton, who ordered his unit's colors bearing the motto *Manus haec inimica tyrannis** "planted on the parapet" while his men "mount[ed] the bank, front[ed] the enemy, and there by word of command [went] through all the ceremony of soldiery, ordering and grounding our arms."

* Adapted from a Latin proverb attributed to Algernon Sydney, an English anti-Royalist politician executed for treason in 1683. The entire proverb reads as follows: *Manus haec inimica tyrannis ense petit placidam sub libertate quietem.* ("This hand, an enemy to tyrants, seeks with the sword calm peace in freedom.")

Not unreasonably, Duncan saw this as "wanton." In fact, both actions were part of the parade within the parade of an army showing off for history, while its putative commander in chief struck poses consistent with the greatness of the occasion.[78]

It was Washington who fired the first allied cannon on the 9th of October. Richard Butler, a diary-packing colonel from Pennsylvania, thought it a great "compliment," a celebration of the general before his army had begun to fight: "This day at 3 o'clock, p.m., the batteries of Lamb and the Marquis de St. Simon opened with great elegance and were quickly followed."[79]

The elegance was a matter of opinion. For Thacher, who "more than once witnessed fragments of the mangled bodies and limbs of British soldiers thrown into the air by . . . our shells," the exhibition verged on the grotesque.[80] Joseph P. Martin, now a sergeant stationed on the British left with "ten heavy guns [and] . . .a bomb battery of three huge mortars," recalled his impatience as he waited for the signal to open the bombardment." It came at noon and was followed by an earth-shaking bombardment by all of the allied guns, firing more or less in unison:

> I was in the trenches the day that the batteries were to be opened. All were upon the tiptoe of expectation and impatience to see the signal given to open the whole line of batteries, which was to be the hoisting of the American flag in the ten-gun [lead-off] battery. About noon, the much-wished-for signal went up. I confess I felt a secret pride swell my heart when I saw the 'star-spangled banner' waving majestically in the very faces of our implacable adversaries. It appeared like an omen of success to our enterprise, and so it proved in reality. A simultaneous discharge of all the guns in the line followed, the French

troops accompanying it with 'Huzza for the Americans!' [81]

For Martin, writing in 1828, the hoisting of the American flag and "Huzzas for the Americans!" were heralds of a star-spangled future as much as they were omens of military success. Though he would shortly be engaged in fierce, hand-to-hand combat for Redoubt 10 (in which he would wield a double ax), he was already laying a claim to history, impatient for the epochal victory.

Ebenezer Denny recorded events as they occurred. Yet even he seemed transported by the grandeur. Cannon fire at night was "brilliant." He did not see shell bursts; he saw "comets." "The scene viewed from the camp was now grand, particularly after dark – a number of shells from the works of both parties passing high in the air, and descending in a curve, each with a long train of fire, exhibited a brilliant spectacle."[82] Thacher's description of the fiery projectiles which set fire to the *Charon*, a 44-gun British ship of the line, and three other vessels at anchor in the York, seems to travel even further from the facts: in his diary, he called the display an instance of the "sublime." "From the bank of the river I had a fine view of this splendid conflagration. The ships were enwrapped in a torrent of fire which spread with vivid brightness along the combustible rigging . . . then ran with amazing rapidity up to the tops of the several masts, while all around was thunder and lightning from our numerous cannon and mortars, and in the darkness of the night, presented one of the most sublime and magnificent spectacles which can be imagined." Even the misses, shells which fell short into the York River, seemed like "spouting sea monsters."[83]

In American accounts of Yorktown, Cornwallis frequently appears as foil to Washington. As the American commander in chief seeks ever more exposed situations to strike poses suited to his heroic stature, Cornwallis is said to live a troglodytic existence in a cave dug in Secretary Thomas Nelson's garden:

> I this day dined [wrote St. George Tucker on October 11, [1781] in company with the Secretary.* He says our Bombardment produced great Effects in annoying the Enemy & destroying their Works . . . Lord Cornwallis has built a kind of Grotto at the foot of the Secretary's garden where he lives under ground – a Negroe of the Secretary's was kill'd in his House. – It seems to be his Opinion that the British are a good deal dispirited altho' he says they affect to say they have no Apprehensions of the Garrison's falling. – An immense number of Negroes have died, in the most miserable Manner in York.[84]

The juxtaposition of Cornwallis in his grotto to Nelson's dead slave might be a narrative accident. But the "immense number" of slaves said to have died "miserably" by St. George Tucker was fire for effect: the British had "liberated" the slaves in their baggage train onto the no-man's land between the two armies, only to disappear down their bolt holes as soon as the cannons roared. In his journal entry for October 12, Tucker fairly characterized this as a crime against humanity.[85] Though all the killing was done by allied guns, such scenes allowed Virginians to gain a much-needed moral leverage.

Meting out glory for the victory got more attention than planning for the attack. The honor of taking Redoubts 9 and 10 (the key to the British left at Yorktown) was accordingly

Gen. Lord Cornwallis "Said to live a troglodytic existence in a cave"

* Secretary Thomas Nelson, the 65-year-old uncle of Gov. Thomas Nelson, was held as a captive in Yorktown during the early days of the seige.

split: The French, led by the Baron de Viomenil, were assigned to take Redoubt 9. The Americans, led by Col. Hamilton (under the command of the Marquis de Lafayette), were given Redoubt 10. The American assault went off as directed at 6:45 p.m.; the French, a half hour later at 7:15 p. m. – an order of battle that all but ensured that the late-starting French would get the worst of it, as they in fact did. Though the French arrived at Redoubt 9 "in perfect order and silence" (according to Jean Baptiste Antoine de Verger, an officer with the Royal Deux Ponts), they found themselves facing a "lively musket fire.":

> We found their abatis* in far better condition than we had anticipated, since much of our artillery had been battering the redoubt for several days. Ignoring the enemy fire and slashing those that resisted with their axes, our pioneers had opened passages for us through which the grenadiers and chasseurs of the Royal Deux-Ponts and Gatinais Regiments entered the fosses together with the . . . pioneers, who were still obliged to cut through several palisades to open the . . . redoubts.[86]

With that, the French climbed onto the parapet of the redoubt, bayoneting anyone who resisted, while graciously sparing the survivors. British casualties amounted to 18 dead and 43 captured. The French, who had 59 killed in the entire siege, lost 46 (with 68 wounded) in this one engagement.[87]

---

* An abatis is "composed of the tops of trees, the small branches cut off with a slanting stroke which renders them as sharp as spikes." These trees are then laid at a small distance from the trench or ditch, pointing outwards, and the butts fastened to the ground in such a manner that they cannot be removed by those on the outside of them. It is almost impossible to get through them. Through these we were to cut a passage before we or the other assailants could enter." Joseph Plumb Martin, *Private Yankee Doodle*, George E. Scheer, ed., (Eastern Acorn Press, 1998), p. 234.

For his part in the assault on Redoubt 10, sapper Joseph Martin was given an axe: "We arrived at the trenches a little before sunset. I saw several officers fixing bayonets on long staves." As soon as it was dark, Martin's brigade crept out of the trenches to await the signal to attack, "three shells with their fiery trains mount[ing] the air in quick succession." Soon he heard the words 'Up up!', whereupon the entire detachment moved silently on toward the redoubt . . with unloaded muskets." The aim was to avoid the accidental firing of a musket which might alert the defenders. But, despite this precaution, the Americans were detected as they reached the abatis and the enemy "opened a sharp fire." At first, Martin thought the British were killing Americans at a great rate, but then he heard, "'The fort's our own!' and 'Rush on Boys!'" At once, Martin and his comrades swarmed over the top. "Our Miners were ordered not to enter the fort but there was no stopping them. 'We will go,' said they. 'Then go to the devil,' said the commanding officer of our corps, 'if you will.'"[88]

Martin's high spirits notwithstanding, the attack was a near-death experience for him: "A man at my side received a ball in his head and fell under my feet, crying out bitterly. . . As I mounted the breastwork, I met an old associate hitching himself down into the trench. I knew him by the light of the enemy's musketry, it was so vivid." Martin's friend and the man who took a ball in the head were later found dead at the bottom of the abatis. Total American losses for the attack on Redoubt 10 were 24 soldiers and four officers, of which only two were killed.[89]

For Thacher the American assault on Redoubt 10 had quasi-mythical significance. It was not only a great feat of arms; it was a triumph of American can-do initiative over old world rigidity: "The cause of the great loss sustained by the French troops . . . was that the American troops when they came to the abatis,

The Storming of Redoubt 10
"The fort's our own!"

removed a part of it with their hands and leaped over the remainder. The French troops . . . waited till their pioneers had cut away the abatis . . . which exposed them longer to the galling fire of the enemy."[90] The French take on all this was, well, predictably French. After they seized Redoubt 9, someone shouted *"Vive le Roi!!"* The British, correctly assuming the redoubt was now in French hands, turned their cannons on it – abruptly ending the celebration. Lafayette deserved at least part of the blame. After Martin and his colleagues took Redoubt 10, recalled Thacher, "The Marquis de Lafayette sent his aid, Major Barbour, through the tremendous fire of the whole line of the British, to inform the Baron de Viomenil, that 'he was in his redoubt, and [to] ask the baron where he was.'" The Major found the Baron waiting for the abatis to be cleared. "Tell the Marquis I am not in mine, but will be in five minutes," he said, and "instantly advanced." The Baron arrived "within his time," Thacher said. In fact, Viomenil arrived early. But to do so he had to literally drive men to their deaths.[91] The day's greatest honor went to Hamilton, who for all his vainglory performed well. For

Lafayette, his commanding officer, the honor of presiding over this glorious assault was more than enough.

The British guns fell silent on the day after the assault on Redoubts 9 and 10. On October 17 (according to Thacher) "not less than one hundred pieces of heavy ordnance" were "in continual operation during the last twenty-four hours." He added, "[the] whole peninsula trembles under the incessant thunderings of our infernal machines; we have leveled some of their works in ruins, and silenced their guns; they have almost ceased firing. We are so near as to have a distinct view of the dreadful havoc and destruction of their works, and even see the men in their lines tore to pieces by the bursting of our shells." The drama was now "drawing to a close."[92] At 11 a.m., Cornwallis sent out an officer and a lone drummer-boy with a flag of truce. He proposed a cessation of hostilities for 24 hours so that the parties could discuss possible terms of capitulation.

Washington accepted the offer, and early the next day, set forth his terms. They were the same terms Cornwallis had imposed on Gen. Benjamin Lincoln at Charleston, with the added humiliation that the offer was delivered by Col. John Laurens, son of Henry Laurens, the American Ambassador to Holland, seized at sea by Cornwallis' brother in October. Cornwallis had two hours to accept. Without food (except for a few putrefying corpses of horses), with a third of his army too sick to fight and his last hope, ferrying his army over to Gloucester, having foundered the night before in a wind, the British general had little hope of getting any better terms. At noon on October 18 he agreed to surrender. His army would march, with its colors cased, out of Yorktown on the following day and ground its arms in a field a mile down the road to Hampton.

Thacher's account of the actual capitulation was framed as a drama of contrasts: "This is to us a most glorious day; but to the British, one of bitter chagrin and disappointment. Preparations are now making to receive as captives that vindictive, haughty commander, and that victorious army, who, by their robberies and murders, have so long been a scourge to our brethren of the Southern states." At 12 p.m., the French and American armies were drawn up in two parallel lines extending a mile on both sides of the main road leading south and west out of Yorktown. The Americans were lined up on the east side of the road, the French on the west. At the ends of the two lines were Washington and Rochambeau with their entire staff. The French were resplendent in white uniforms, displaying "a martial and noble appearance." The Americans were dirty and unkempt in threadbare wool and linen. Yet, said Thacher, every one of them "exhibited an erect, soldierly air, and every countenance beamed with satisfaction and joy." Largely ignored by historians, but crucial to the filmic, epochal nature of the event, were the "prodigious" crowds of spectators which "in point of numbers" were said to be at least equal in size to the two armies. Despite the presence of 30,000 soldiers and spectators, "universal silence and order prevailed."[93]

This "immense concourse" then had to wait two hours before the British, now cast in the role of "the captive army" by Thacher, slowly filed out of the breach in the redoubt. "Every eye was prepared," said Thacher, to gaze on Cornwallis, an "object of peculiar interest." But Cornwallis was not there. In his place he had sent Maj. Gen. O'Hara, elegantly mounted and leading the "conquered troops" in "a slow and solemn step, with shouldered arms, colors cased and drums." The legend that the British army marched to "The World Turned Upside Down" is just that – a legend, though in defeating the British, it seemed to Americans that that was what they had done. Still, like most myths it expressed a truth:

for Americans, accession to the status of a nation; for the British, a metaphor of bewilderment and shock.[94]

When O'Hara reached the end of the column of British and American soldiers, he tried to offer his sword to Rochambeau. The Comte merely nodded to Washington. O'Hara then turned to Washington and apologized for the absence of Cornwallis. "With his usual dignity and politeness, [Thacher later recalled] his excellency pointed to Maj. Gen. Lincoln for directions, by whom the British army was conducted into a spacious field where it was intended they should ground their arms."[95] Thacher was willing to grant the "decent and neat appearance [of the British soldiers] as respects arms and clothing," but that was only because Cornwallis had "opened his store" of clothing and equipment. Otherwise, the British appeared "disorderly and unsoldierly . . . their step . . . irregular, and their ranks frequently broken."[96]

But it was in the field, when they came to the last act of the drama [Thacher continued] that the spirit and pride of the British soldier was put to the severest test: here

The Surrender of Cornwallis
"The Conte nodded to Washington"

their mortification could not be concealed. Some of the platoon officers appeared to be exceedingly chagrined when giving the word '*ground arms*,' and . . . performed this duty in a very unofficer-like manner; and that many of the soldiers manifested a *sullen temper*, throwing their arms on the pile with violence, as if determined to render them useless. This irregularity, however, was checked by the authority of General Lincoln.[97] (Italics in original.)

Once disarmed, the British soldiers (all 3,456 of them) "were conducted back to Yorktown, and guarded by our troops till they could be removed to the place of their destination" which for most was rural Maryland, Virginia or western Pennsylvania.[98] There, more than a few of them, particularly the Hessians, would put down roots, electing to become citizens when the war ended in 1783. The officers were paroled to British-occupied New York; there, they soon found ships to England.

For Thacher, Cornwallis' absence from Surrender Field was deeply disappointing. But if the point was to humiliate the British army's most celebrated general, that was under way. "I have the mortification [Cornwallis wrote Gen. Clinton] to inform you that I have been forced to give up the posts of York and Gloucester, and to surrender the troops under my command." It was only the first maneuver in what was to be a life-long battle to disclaim responsibility for a disaster he had foreseen too well.[99]

News of Cornwallis' surrender reached the Pall Mall home of Lord George Germain, Secretary of State for the Colonies, at noon on November 25, 1781. He received it with shock and horror:

Lord Walsingham* . . . happened to be there [Nathaniel

* A former Chief Justice.

Wraxall recalled] when the messenger brought the news. Without communicating to any other person [Germain] immediately got with him into a hackney-coach and drove to Lord Stormont's [Secretary of State for the Northern Department] residence in Portland Place. Having imparted to him the disastrous information and taken him into the carriage, they instantly proceeded to [Lord Chancellor Thurlow's] house in . . .Bloomsbury, whom they found at home. . . [A]fter a short consultation, they determined to lay it themselves in person before [the Prime Minister] Lord North . . . [T]hey arrived at his door in Downing Street between one and two o'clock. [North's] firmness, and even his presence of mind, which had withstood the [Gordon] riots of 1780, gave way for a short time under this awful disaster. I asked Lord George afterwards how he took the communication when made to him. 'As he would have taken a ball to his breast,' . . . he opened his arms, exclaiming wildly, as he paced up and down the apartment, repeating 'O God! It is all over!' many times under emotions of the deepest consternation and distress."[100]

The King, informed by a note from Germain, showed his usual "calmness, dignity and . . . self command." At dinner that evening, Lord George enlarged on the significance of the defeat. It meant, he said, "the termination of this great contest between England and America" – the word "great" signifying what he would say later: that it was the loss of a war that presaged the loss of an empire.[101]

For Washington, who had spent the siege atop a parapet amid "cannon[fire] and musketry," Yorktown was the long hoped-for vindication – a complete answer to the critics (and there were still many) who doubted his military judgment. But surely the sweetest moment of the surrender was Rochambeau's nod to O'Hara. Here was proof that a role he had merely inhabited, Allied commander in chief, was now truly his. During the battle Washington's aide, Col. Cobb, had said, "Sir, you are too much exposed here. Had you not better step a little back?" "Colonel Cobb," Washington is said to have replied, "if you are afraid you have liberty to step back." In stories like this, the myth of his unflappable poise grew until it petrified into marble and the immortal moment lengthened into undying fame.[102]

The Yorktown campaign was not the greatest triumph of George Washington's life. But it did lay the foundation for his George III-given character as "the greatest man in the world." Rochambeau's fool, the anxiety-ridden diarist making his case to a future board of inquiry, the child jumping for joy on a wharf in Chester, followed by the return of the commander in chief – these were

King George III
"With his usual calmness, dignity and self-command"

glimpses, not so much of the real Washington, but of an em-battled, histrionic personality which achieved integration by enacting ever more heroic parts in ever more difficult situations. A test of his new-found mythic identity was to come on March 16, 1783 when, in what Joseph Ellis has called "the Last Temp-tation of Washington,"[103] he foiled a threatened coup d'etat by his own officers (the Newburgh Conspiracy) with a pair of eye-glasses and the simple statement that it was hard for him to read the speech he had prepared as he had grown "blind in the serv-ice of my country."[104] The same theatrical ideas were on offer in his last Circular Letter to the States in June of 1783 when, in prose now called "poignant" and "lyrical," he described himself and his fellow citizens as "[a]ctors on a most conspicuous The-atre, which seems to be peculiarly designed by Providence for the display of human greatness and felicity."[105] Finally, on December 22nd of that year, in what he assumed would be his farewell to public life, he noted his "retirement" from "the great Theatre of Action."[106]

In this age, such language would inspire sneers; then, it inspired patriotic tears. In fact, Washington had not only acted *a* part; he had acted the *best* parts, for all the right reasons: duty, honor and integrity. Whatever got in the way – Congress' con-sternation, his own anxieties – simply had to be endured. An imperfect man, he would spend his entire life practicing to be great until finally he became just that. So it was that each per-formance had to exceed the last, had to display ever greater feats of will-power until the performer finally left "the stage of life" to enjoy a death-in-life immortality as the best portrayer of *himself*.

Speaking of Gilbert Stuart's portrait of Washington on the dol-lar bill, journalist Richard Brookhiser has noted that "[h]e is in our textbooks, and our wallets but not our hearts."[107] Lady Liston's Washington and the Washington of Morris' anecdote dare us to love a dead man. No more than dignified, honored and rich – that was what George Washington had set out to be: to overcome his passions, which Morris described as "tumul-tuous," "almost too mighty for man."[108] That he succeeded in this we owe to his fierce self-command and equally fierce desire for fame. The cruel irony, one he has yet to escape, is that he was not born to play the stoic. He was born to play the impulsive boy, jumping for joy, or the rabid rebel, thundering sedition to Arthur Lee. The face that "never yet betrayed its feelings" was a complete fiction.

That we find no pathos in this has more to do with our own

ideas than Washington's. The letter below was written by Washington only moments after he took his final leave of Lafayette. Unlike his much-revised diary and the letters he wrote to office-seekers and political allies, it is astonishingly unguarded, not (as some scholars have claimed) because Lafayette was "the child he never had," but because their emotional leave-taking had revived the youth in Washington that might have been the father of the man.

> I called to mind the days of my youth, & found they had long since fled to return no more; that I was now descending the hill, I had 52 years been climbing – & that tho' I was blessed with a good constitution, I was of a short lived family – and might soon expect to be entombed in the drear mansions of my father's – These things darkened the shades & gave a gloom to the picture . . . but I will not repine – I have had my day.

It was a valediction, not a mourning, an old man's evocation of death cut short by an intervention of control, as Washington went from thinking about what might have been to remembering who he was.[109] We have not lost his idea of greatness; but we have lost the world that gave it meaning. To compare Washington to a movie star, to call him a dead white male, or ridicule his efforts to master himself is to suggest just how debased our ideas of greatness have become. Here was a fallible man who set out to be great; who, as a gift to his nation, became just that. We do not honor a marble Washington; we honor the tight-lipped Washington of Stuart's portraits, still struggling to stifle the unbidden impulse, still proving to us that greatness in any age can be achieved only by relentless acts of self-denial and that what we call character is *always* a facade.

The Man Behind the Face

It is interesting to find that Washington attended a play on the evening of the day he took Patcy Custis to see Dr. Arthur Lee.* Unfortunately, Washington failed to note its name. It was probably not the most popular musical comedy of the era, the *Beggar's Opera* by John Gay, which (according to an advertisement in Rind's *Virginia Gazette*) was to open a month later. But it might have been *The Orphan, or the Unhappy Marriage*, advertised in Rind's *Gazette* as a "tragedy" opening on Friday, April 15, and, apparently, scheduled to run for more than one night. If it was *The Orphan*, it had to share the bill with a "new Comic Dance, call'd *The Bedlamites*," performed by the Bedlamite and his "Mad Doctor." If the idea of a lunatic cutting a figure while being pursued by his no less demented doctor did not quite suit Washington's taste, there was the newly-added entr'acte, a pantomime entitled *Harlequin Skeleton, or the Burgomaster Trick'd.*¹¹⁰

Washington's love of the theater has been noted by virtually every commentator, with one historian, Paul Longmore, calculating that "[on] a typical visit to Williamsburg

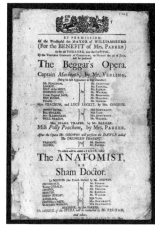

A playbill for
The Beggar's Opera
"The most popular musical
comedy of the era"

* See pp. 9–10, infra.

in June 1770, [Washington] attended performances of the American Company of Comedians [a traveling theater company] five out of seven nights. When the roving troupes came closer to Mount Vernon, he traveled to see them at Alexandria, Dumfries, Fredericksburg and Annapolis. Throughout the 1760s and 1770s, he attended the theatre avidly."[111] In fact, Washington enjoyed all kinds of plays, from satires like George Farquhar's *The Recruiting Officer* to Shakespearean tragedies. His favorite play was Joseph Addison's *The Tragedy of Cato*, the story of the noble Roman who commits suicide rather than submit to the iniquities of Caesar. Though Congress prohibited theatergoing during the war years, Washington ordered the staging of *The Tragedy of Cato* for his men at Valley Forge, no doubt intending (as one scholar has suggested) "to improve the soldiers' morale by inspiring them with the example of Cato's men who had demonstrated extreme selflessness in the struggle for liberty." After the war, Washington would again rely on Cato's example of "unexampled patriotism and virtue" in putting down a mutiny of his officers.[112]

It has been suggested that Washington "derived a sense of identity and purpose from his emulation of Cato."[113] And in fact it is the rare scholarly study of Washington that does not at least suggest that *The Tragedy of Cato* could be the key to unlocking the great man's soul. But in fact the only role in *Cato* that Washington is on record as wanting to play is that of Prince Juba, who rashly "opens the weakness of his soul" (his love for Cato's daughter Marcia), only to be informed by her father that he has lessened himself by not speaking only of "conquest or death." It was thus the character of the impulsive Juba, not of Cato, which first attracted Washington's notice; not to turn the conversation toward conquest or death but to provide cover for an impulsive avowal of love to Sally Fairfax, the wife of his old friend, George William Fairfax.[114] The affair that was not an affair was broached by Washington in two chaotic love letters, both written at a low point in British-American fortunes in the French and Indian War.

In the first letter, written the day before the ill-fated British assault on Fort Duquesne, Washington professes himself "a Votary to love" only to admit that there is "a lady in the case." In the second, written 13 days later, he sets aside lovemaking to report on the results of the battle. (Six of the eight officers and 62 of the 168 enlisted men in Washington's regiment were killed.) The two letters are presented together, with the sounds of war relegated to a footnote.[115] This may save paper, but it makes it harder to grasp the growing sense of desperation behind one of the most tortuous, if not torturously honest confessions Washington ever made:

Sally Fairfax
"The lady in the case"

> Dear Madam
>   Camp at Fort Cumberland, 12th Septr. 1758.

Yesterday I was honourd with your short, but very agreeable favour of the first Instt. how joyfully I catch at the happy occasion of renewing a Corrispondance which I feard was disrelishd on your part, I leave to time, that never failing Expositor of All things. – and to a Monitor equally as faithful in my own Breast, to Testifie. In silence I now express my Joy. – Silence which in some cases – I wish the present – speaks more Intelligably than the sweetest Eloquence.

If you allow that any honour can be derivd from my opposition to Our present system of management, you destroy the merit of it entirely in me by attributing my anxiety to the animating prospect of possessing Mrs. Custis. When – I need not name it. – guess it yourself. – Shoud not my own Honour, and Country's welfare be the excitement? Tis true, I profess myself a Votary to Love – I acknowledge that a Lady is in the Case – and further I confess that this Lady is known to you. – Yes Madam, as well as she is to one, who is too sensible of her Charms to deny the Power, whose Influence he feels and must ever Submit to. I feel the force of her amiable beauties in the recollection of a thousand tender passages that I could wish to obliterate, till I am bid to revive them. – but experience alas! Sadly reminds me how Impossible this is. – and evinces an opinion which I have long entertained, that there is a Destiny, which has the Sovereign Controul of our Actions – not to be resisted by the Strongest efforts of Human Nature.

You have drawn me my dear Madam, or rather have I drawn myself, into an honest confession of a Simple Fact – misconstrue not my meaning – 'tis obvious – doubt it not, nor expose it, – the World has no business to know the object of my Love, declard in this manner to you – you when I want to conceal it – One thing, above all things in this World I wish to know, and only one person of your Acquaintance can solve me that, or guess my meaning. – but adieu to this, till happier times, if I shall ever see them . . .

* * * * *

Dear Madam

Camp at Rays Town, 25th Septr 1758

Do we still misunderstand the true meaning of each others Letters? I think it must appear so, tho I would

feign hope the contrary as I cannot speak plainer without
– but I'll say no more, and leave you to guess the rest . . .
I should think my time more agreeable spent believe me,
in playing a part in Cato with Company you mention, &
myself doubly happy in being the Juba to such a Marcia
as you must make . . .

One historian has attributed the convolutions in these letters to Washington's intense discomfort with "the act of
writing" and because he felt compelled to use "elliptical language" to avoid prying eyes. Another finds this sort of romantic
banter typical of the age. In fact, neither is right. As we have
seen, the character Washington is most comfortable when he is
acting *that part*. Here, he is speaking passionately, for himself,
and the effect on his syntax is as predictable as his message.
Instead of a simple "I love you," Sally is given a confession
"drawn from himself" (as in "drawing a tooth"), the pain of
stifling an avowal of love being, for Washington, equivalent to
the thing itself. If this seems unduly paradoxical, we need to
remember that the Washington of the Sally letters is the first
incarnation of a President who has recently been described as
a "consummate actor [but not] a poseur [who] kept his per-
formance understated" to allay fears that he would
"manipulate passions."[116]

Washington had other reasons, besides a need for secrecy, to
avoid an avowal. Making love to his best friend's wife was
clearly at odds with the Washington value system. Nor was
Sally a coy virgin to be seduced merely by hearing herself
called the lady in the case. Add to this the fact that Washington
was writing from a war camp on the eve of a battle. How does
a man anticipating violent death register a torrid passion for his
best friend's wife? If his name is George Washington, he
expresses joy " in silence," doubts whether that applies "in the

present case," then seeks to stifle his rising passion with fierce interventions of control. Instead of a simple "I love you," Washington enacts the tension between saying and not saying, firing off dashes and exclamation marks in an explosive salute to emotions too great for words. It is a forced, not a free declaration, in which the clichés of fashionable love are forced to run a gauntlet of explosive interjections, and careering clauses. Less an avowal than a renunciation of love, it must have seemed to Sally a rather odd confession – made no less odd surely by this white Virginia planter taking on the role of "Juba, *an African* Prince."[117] At the same time, *Cato*'s odd mix of histrionics and repressed feelings was exactly the right vehicle for revealing a forbidden passion for the wife of an old friend. And there were other, purely contextual reasons why the role of Juba appealed to Washington. As Marcia's would-be lover, as the military leader of one of Rome's chief allies, as a one-man chorus to the Cato, Juba is both integral to the play and its principal commentator. The effect of this transfer of authorial prerogatives within the *Cato* is to allow would-be players of the role unusual freedom when it comes to interpreting Juba's place in the world of the play.

That Washington equated Juba's "smothered fondness" for Marcia with his own stifled avowal to Sally should be obvious to anyone who has bothered to read the letters quoted above. Unfortunately, tone deaf readings of *Cato* are too often the launching point for misreadings of Washington the man. Most readers of Washington's favorite play get the sexual innuendo of Juba's "big passion" "swelling for a vent," but not all of them and, one gathers, virtually none of the myth-keepers.[118] The language is quite explicit: Marcia is "surprised" into an avowal of love that sounds like the act of sexual intercourse itself, "[breaking] through its weak restraints, and burn[ing] in its full luster." Nor should we be surprised when Juba says he is "lost in ecstasy" or that he calls this "life indeed." There would of course be no breaking through for Washington with Sally, no mutual avowal of love and no signal from Mrs. Fairfax that her would-be Prince Juba could ever hope to be lost in ecstasy. That said, the Sally letters leave no doubt as to the nature or intensity of Washington's feelings. In place of an elegant *billet doux*, Sally is given broken syntax signifying raw sexual passion. Instead of an avowal of love she is shown a titanic struggle to achieve self-mastery. Those who wish to believe that Washington was "passionately in love with Sally" will no doubt continue to rely on the Sally letters to argue their case; but the case is ultimately an apposite one, as it rests on the assumption of a fifth columnist in the soul of Washington, nurturing, as Joseph Ellis puts it, an "undercurrent of passion in the most notorious model of self control in all of American history."[119] As Washington's friends noted after his death, passion was as true to his nature as his sense of honor and need for fame, making the character of Washington a deeply-taxing work in progress. Poker-faced he could clearly be. But he was also, in Ellis' words, "possessed [of a] deep seated capacity to feel powerful emotions," with a lifelong interest in the drama of renunciation and desire.

Cato, we need to remember, is a tragedy. What is more, it is a tragedy riddled with irony. The "stern, and awful as a God" Cato of the play's last act is a *dying* Cato, who is said not to "know how to wink at human frailty, / Or pardon weakness that he never felt." It is not Cato, but the usurper and dictator Caesar, who is said to have "the virtues of humanity." The famous line, "Thy life is not thy own, when Rome demands it" (which has been described as "flawlessly exemplif[ying] patriotic virtue") is uttered by Cato over the dead body of his son – an act of such astonishing unnaturalness that Juba is moved to wonder, "Was ever man like this!"[120] In short, if Cato is indeed the hero of *The Tragedy of Cato*, he is an oddly perverse one and his virtues, celebrated though they might be in Washington's army, are the virtues of a man dead to life.

And herein lies the final irony of *The Tragedy of Cato*. Instead of a flawless model of patriotic virtue, Cato is portrayed as an unnatural, self-deluded fanatic. "Alas!" he cries, as the final "beam of light breaks in" on him, "I fear I've been too hasty."[121] Was Washington alive to *Cato's* deadly irony? Did a "beam of light" ultimately break in on him? We cannot be sure. We know only that Washington's own portrayal of stoic self-abnegation is tied to Juba, not Cato, and that sexual innuendo was part of the act. Discovered en route to the theater in Williamsburg, sporting "a pleasant, but in serious matters somewhat grave countenance" (in keeping with Rule Nineteen of his famous Rules of Civility), Washington could no more be said to be free of irony than he could be said to be fully at peace.[122] He was not Cato. But he was not Juba either. He looked calm, but he was at war with himself. Only in 1798, with his apotheosis firmly in view, did he reopen "the weakness of his soul" to Sally. The scene was Mount Vernon, transported to Italy by a hackneyed Virgilian allusion to his "fig and vine." The show of classical erudition was for Sally – a gentle reminder (in case she needed one) that he had done pretty well for a simple Virginia farmer.[123]

My Dear Madam:

Five and twenty years, nearly, have passed since I have considered myself as permanent resident of this place [Mount Vernon]; or have been in a situation to indulge myself in a familiar intercourse with my friends, by letter or otherwise. –

During this period, so many important events have occurred, and such changes in men and things have taken place, as the compass of a letter would give you but an inadequate idea of. None of which events, however, nor all of them together, have been able to eradicate from my mind, the recollection of those happy moments, the happiest of my life, which I have enjoyed in your company. –

Worn out in a manner by the toils of my past labour, I am again seated under my Vine & Fig tree, and wish I could add that there are none to make us afraid; but those whom we have been accustomed to call our good friends and allies, are endeavouring , if not to make us afraid, yet to despair of our property, are provoking us to Acts of self defence, which may lead to war. What will be the result of such measures, time, that faithful expositor of all things, must disclose. –

My wish is to spend the remainder of my days (which cannot be many) in amusements free from those cares from which responsibility is never exempt. –

It had been nearly forty years since he had "bid adieu to happier times," yet his feelings for Sally had endured. He was not dead to life after all.

Properly read, the dash-strewn Sally letters can tell us how Washington felt as well as what he thought; but only if we are alert to their subtext of thwarted sexual passion. Idolaters and those used to treating words as artifacts may find this sort of analysis distasteful. But we need to remember that it is Washington himself who raises the issue of interpretation: "Do we still misunderstand the true meaning of each other's Letters?" he asks Sally, "I think it must appear so, tho I would feign hope the contrary as I cannot speak plainer without – but I'll say no more, and leave you to guess the rest."[124] To be sure, Washington is not addressing us. He is speaking to Sally, who clearly enjoyed great advantages as a close reader of his letters. That said, the continuing controversy over these letters suggests that Washington's best efforts to repress an illicit passion for his best friend's wife have not gone unnoticed, only under-estimated. The issue is no longer whether the private letters of a taciturn Virginian by the name of George Washington are sometimes open to interpretation; but whether, like most writing, they should always be.

Why *did* Washington choose Arthur Lee to receive his treasonous declaration? They were not good friends; nor, as far as we know, even very good acquaintances. Here was a man (Washington) who never took a friend without trying him severely confiding treasonous sentiments to a man he barely knew and a notorious malcontent at that. If it were true, as Lee charged, that the British government was plotting "to sap, not storm America's freedoms," Washington's decision to confide his seditious views to Lee was downright reckless.[125] Was it that, with the table cleared, the port going round and the conversation turning to politics, the irrational suspicions which Benjamin Franklin would later cite as proof of Lee's "sick mind" became the occasion for an exchange of extreme utterances, each more inflammatory than the last? Was it Lee's determination to support the cause of liberty with his last breath that won Washington's confidence? Did he find a companion for his own thoughts in Lee's histrionic utterances? (One is tempted to say that the more extreme Arthur Lee sounded, the more Washington liked it.)

We may never know. But if Arthur Lee is ever invited up to the big house of American history, someone may notice that his claim to scholarly notice rests on the same basis as other Virginians – that his magisterial airs and irritability were shared by George Washington, a man with a big passion and such an exaggerated sense of grievance as to qualify him on that basis alone as the leader of a rebellion. In short, if the story of George Washington is well known, his state of mind is not. Under perpetual siege from what was has been called "the most ungovernable passions," Washington can hardly be called a reluctant convert to resistance. He was already there. Short-tempered by nature, he would spend the rest of his life trying to become what he was not. The Washington we honor on the one dollar bill is Washington after peace has been restored, resignedly bearing on his face the look of a man who has posed too long for his portrait. Friends also saw him that way. Jefferson emphasized his statuesque bearing, describing it as "exactly [as] . . . one would wish, his deportment easy, erect and noble." Abigail Adams compared him (with help from John Dryden) to an entire "temple/Sacred by birth, and built by hands divine . . . the pile [not] unworthy of the God." Nor was the effect lost when the pile moved: "the most graceful figure . . . on horseback," said Jefferson.[126]

George Washington having become a genuine American hero in his own time, would-be biographers have had little to do but polish up the marble and keep the birds away. Thus we are told by one writer in a rare, refreshing effort at humor that Washington's friends and family "witnessed and esteemed in him a self mastery they could only term as *Cato*-tonic."[127] But it turns out the joke is on us, not only for misinterpreting Washington's interest in *Cato*, the tragedy, but for failing to allow for the possibility that he was alive to the play's bitterest irony – that the austere stoicism of Cato was unnatural, not admirable – and not sustainable in real life. It is our good fortune that Washington never lost control; that he was always what he seemed. It is our bad fortune to be obliged to perpetuate a myth that is so damaging to his humanity. What we ought to admire is not the iconically-composed Washington of Gilbert Stuart but the authentic savage of Jean-Antoine Houdon.

Houdon's Bust of Washington
"His oaths made the leaves tremble
on the trees"

A *Yorktown Memoir**

The mythic nature of the event that won the American Revolution is not wholly lost on us. Recapturing the sense of wonder of those who were there is less easy, but if anything can, it is the letters below, which remind us that this was an epoch as well as a moment in time and that some things are simply beyond history.

To
Joseph Lyon Esqre
Wester Ogil Manor
near Baltimore

My Honourable Sir & Father —
Once more I beg to inform you that all is well with me, and I Hope both yourself & my mother are enjoying a like Good Health. Last night Genl Lincoln opened a long line of parallel Works to the British, and now my lord Cornwallis will never march out of Yorktown except with cased colors, unless Sir Henry [Clinton] comes to his aide with the Fleat, which is most unlikely. With the French we

* "Memories of Yorktown," William and Mary College Quarterly Historical Magazine (now William and Mary Quarterly, 2nd Series), Vol. XV, No. 2. (Oct., 1906), published with the permission of the Earl Gregg Swem Library, College of William & Mary and pursuant to a Creative Commons Attribution-ShareAlike 3.0 Unported License.

have 12,000 men in Camp besides the French Fleet. General Washington is expected in Camp to-day, he having been to visit the count De Grasse. You will remember I wrote you before of my friend and Tent mate Lieut. Falvey Fraser, and how I carried him off the field when he was so badly wounded at Germantown four years ago. Well a few days ago he told me some of his past life. I had always thought he was a Virginian. That afternoon I had ridden out below the Camp in the Direction of the York [River]. I had gone about a mile when I saw Falvey coming across a meadow on my right, so I stopped and waited for him. He is a splendid Horseman, and that afternoon the perfect union of horse and rider as they came straight across the field was beautiful to see. While I was waiting somebody suddenly begun to sing on my left. I looked around but saw no one. It seemed to come from a thicket of Pines about two hundred yards away. The song marvelously sweet & clear brought to mind the last time we went to church together, for it was soft and plaintive as a Hymn and not such a Song as one commonly hears in Camp. Though I was close & the Voice was clear I could not understand the words. I happened to glance at Falvey's face & was struck by his rapt attention – he sat there on his Horse as still as a dead man on a summer afternoon & but for the throbbing veins on his forehead and the breathing of his Horse with no more sine of Life. Then the Song stopped and as the last soft notes died away a boyish man in a lieut's uniform of the British army rode out from the Pines. Seeing us he raised his cap & laughed, and then he spurred his horse through the Pines. I pulled my Pistol to shoot him, but Falvey caught my arm and it went off in the air.

Seeing he must explain he drew a long breath and said: 'That was [my] brother & this is the first time I've seen him for five years. That was an old Latin Hymn he was singing. Mother use[d] to sing us to sleep with it in our old home in the Scottish Highlands. I have thought several times past that you wondered greatly about my past life, and now I will tell you what little there is to tell, for you are the only Friend I have in America.

Our family is an old one in Scotland and have lived at Castle Fraser in Aberdeenshire since the twelfth cen. I'll pass over my early life to my college days at Edinburg. After I went there I met a Lady who was visiting there and immediately fell in love with her. To me she was the Paragon of the Female sex. We became engaged and all went well till my brother Henry came to the University. He met Margaret, and from that day my hopes were doomed. We are entirely unlike. He is Clever and Witty and with a face as handsome as Appolloes, while I am Quiet as you know. Before many more Weeks Margaret grew colder and colder to me and encouraged Henry more. About a month before I was to graduate She broke our vows. I was insane at losing her and went to Henry and accused him of acting dishonourably toward me. He resented it and said the Lady surely had a right to choose. Other words passed & I was so angry I snatched a pair of rapiers from the Wall and pitching him one, I made a savage lunge at him, piercing his shoulder. At this moment our older brother Sir Francis, who is an officer with Lord Rodney on the Formidable, rushed in and separated us & lectured me soundly. Then came the revulsion of Feeling at attacking my Brother. I did not want to see their Happiness & not caring what became of me I packed my Books and sailed the next week to America & landed at Yorktown yonder over 5 years ago. I have Relatives here in Virginia, and went to them till I joined the army in the

beginning of the War. I have never heard from across the
Sea since I came over here & did not know that Harry was
in the army. Falvey stopped and seemed to wander away
in thought to some distant place & we rode on in Silence.

I tell you all this, My Dear Sir, because I have since
learned that the Lady who was false to my friend is a distant cousin of ours – Margaret Lyon of Easter Ogil. News
came to-day that Lord Rawdon, who was on his way to
South Carolina has been captured with some Important
papers, by the French fleet.

The People in this Section have been much opress'd
by Lord Cornwallis and Tarleton & there is great
Rejoicing now that we have the Thieving Foxes in the
Den. I hope to be Able to say next Time that the British
have Surrendered: they can't hold out much Longer. With
the Greatest Respect & Affection to yourself & my
mother I am your most Dutiful Son —

Jam[e]s Lyon

Camp before Yorktown,
Octr. 17, 1781.
To
Jos. Lyon, Esqre
Wester Ogil Manor,
near Baltimore.

My Honourable Sir & Father –

I beg to inform you that I am still Alive, and that the
End is nigh, for my Lord C. sent Us a Flag at ten o'clock
this forenoon. All Day yesterday the Guns kept up such a
Thunder that it might be thought Jove Himself was wag-
ing War; and our Solid Shotes have torn their Works to
Peaces. On the night of the 14th: Inst. We stormed and

took two of their Redoubts. One of the storming Partys was Commanded by Comte de Deuponts and the other one – my party [—] by Colo. Alexander Hamilton. The darkness was Intense & we carried them with the Bayonets. The Army is much Joy'd at the success, but I am sad at heart, and I will tell you why. That afternoon Falvey told me that he had a presentiment that something was going to Happen. I tried to laugh it off, but I saw him go to his Mare Beauty and caress her for some time. They had the greatest affection for each other I ever saw, and she would rub her nose against his arm and whin[n]y when he was talking to her, just like she understood Him. That afternoon I heard him say: 'We have been sweethearts, Beauty, we two.' Then he sighed and added tenderly: 'I wish we could go together.' He then put the saddle on and galloped away, and did not come back till Dark. Then after night fell we made ready to creep up on the British. Just before we got to their Sentry I heard the now familiar words of the old Latin Hymn rise full and sweet from behind the Redoubt. Falvey clutched my arm, and I felt him shake like he had a severe chill. In a few moments we were on their works and fighting heavily. I tried to keep near Falvey & as we climbed the mound of Earth and Barrels I saw him plunge his sword into the Breast of a man that stood above Him and the fellow exploded his Pistol in Falvey's face. Just then they set off some Rockets and I saw that the man was Lieut' Fraser. He reeled and dropped his Pistol. Falvey recognized him too and sprung forward and clasped him in his arms and cried 'Harry! Harry! It is I your Brother.' Then both fell to the ground and when I seperated them Lieut' Fraser was dead and Falvey was unconscious from the Pistol shot.

We carried him back to camp, and when we dressed his

wound he was conscious and said to me 'I did my Duty Jim but 't was hard. Don't do too much, I don't want to get well.' Soon after this he sank into a stupor. About sundown the next Day, the 15th, he roused up and said as he felt my hand, 'Listen Jim! don't you hear the old Ave Maria? Its Harry on the way thro' the Parke to the castle. I must hurry and overtake Him.' He then became quiet again.

About eleven o'clock that evening I was sitting with him, when I heard rapid Hoof beats coming. They stopped before our Tent and I heard Beauty whin[n]y. She knew the way for Falvey often left her standing there. After being neglected all Day she had come to hunt Him. He heard her too and started up in Bed saying, 'Whoa Beauty, steady sweetheart, I'm ready.' He groped for the Reigns and his foot was partly raised as though for the stirrup. 'Go Beauty!' he said and sank back in my arms. When I laid him down he was Dead. The mare had heard his last command & Galloped on. The Hoof beats grew fainter till I heard a Sentry challenge & a shot when they stopped. I knew it was as Falvey wished. He and Beauty went together. I miss Him soe for He was the best Friend I had.

I don't know where We will go when Lord C. surrenders. May bee up thro' Maryland and then I'll see you and my mother. With Respects from your

Affec'te & Dutiful Son,
James Lyon

According to *The Historical Register of Virginians in the Revolution*, the writer of the two letters above, James Lyon, was a Lieutenant in Gen. Thomas Nelson's Virginia Light Dragoons.[128] His tent mate at Yorktown was one Lt. Falvey

Fraser of the 14th Regiment of the Virginia Line. Muster Reports for the 14th list a "Lt. Fraser" as a member of Capt. John Marks' company, adding that he was "supposedly killed" at Germantown on Oct. 4, 1777.[129] This error was later corrected by the editor of the *Register* who cites the first letter to prove that Falvey Fraser was rescued wounded from the battlefield by James Lyon only to be "mortally wounded by his own brother, an officer of the British army at Yorktown, Oct 14, 1781,"[130] The *Catalogue of Revolutionary Soldiers . . . To Whom Land Bounty Rights Were Granted* indicates that the Virginia Legislature awarded one Thomas Fraser, Falvey Fraser's heir, 2,666 acres of land for his services in the Revolutionary War.[131] Another source, *The Old New Kent County: Some Account of the Planters, Plantations and Places* records the probate of a Will for Falvey Fraser, dated June 3, 1776. The will names his two brothers, Thomas and William, as executors, and directs that his property be divided among William's children, Falvey* and Susan, his mother (his father being dead) and three sisters, Mary, Anne and Susanna Richeson It seems that this Falvey Fraser was the son of William Fraser, the owner of Sandy Point plantation, Northern a sizable Virginia property of 900 acres lying along the Mattaponi River.[132]

According to British returns of the killed, wounded and missing at Yorktown, a "Lt. Frazer" (first name not given) was among those killed from the 71st Regiment of Foot. It remains to be shown whether this Lt. Fraser was Lt. Henry Fraser, brother of Falvey Fraser; that Henry was one of the defenders of Redoubt 10; and that his brother participated in the American assault. We do know that there were 300 officers and

---

* U.S. Army enlistment records for 1811 show that this Falvey Fraser enlisted, at age 20, as a Private in Capt. Humphrey's company. A series of courts-martial for various offenses followed by a series of reenlistments distinguish his record.

men from the 71st Regiment (the "Fraser Highlanders") among the surrendered British forces at Yorktown; and that they were raised at Stirling, Inverness and Glasgow and served at Boston, Savannah, Charleston, Camden, Guilford Court House and the Siege of Yorktown.

An introductory note to the first printing of the letters in the *William and Mary Quarterly* says that the letters were found in a garret at Wester Ogil, Mercer County, Kentucky, "in a great cedar chest" that had "followed the fortunes of the Lyon family since they left Perth." A search of Kentucky towns of the 18th century has failed to produce any mention of a "Wester Ogil", nor is there evidence of a plantation called "Wester Ogil Manor" in the Baltimore, Maryland area. There is a Joseph Lyon (James' Lyon's father?) listed in a 1775 colonial census of Charles County, Maryland, and a James Lyon in the 1790 and 1810 federal censuses for Mercer County Kentucky. In short, though it seems reasonable to assume that the Lyons of Wester Ogil, Baltimore and Mercer County, Kentucky were related to the Lyons of Wester Ogil, Angus, Scotland, that has yet to be proved.

Much of what we would like to know about Falvey Fraser, Henry Fraser, James Lyon and the ostensibly fickle Margaret Lyon may never be known. We may assume, based on long-standing practice, that Falvey was buried along with the other American dead somewhere on the battlefield of Yorktown and that Henry was interred where he fell, at the bottom of Redoubt 10. Redoubt 10 having long since washed out to sea, Henry's remains are happily beyond the reach of the most diligent scholarship. For the rest – the brothers' conflict over Margaret Lyon, the old Latin hymn that alerted Falvey to Henry's presence at Yorktown, the eerie coincidence of their meeting at Redoubt 10 and Beauty's sad death – the reader is on her own.

Notes

1   Lee's thesis, "*Experiments on the* Peruvian *Bark*, by Arthur Lee, *M.D.*,"
can be found online at the Royal Society's website at *Phil. Trans.* January 1, 1766, 56: 95–104; doi:10.1098/rstl.1766. For Patcy's visit to
Lee, see Washington's Cash Accounts ledger in W.W. Abbot and
Dorothy Twohig, eds., *The Papers of George Washington, Colonial Series
(1744–1775)*, (10 vols., Charlottesville, VA 1983–95) 8: 78, (hereafter
"*Papers, Colonial Series*"). Washington's ledger shows that the payment to Dr. Lee was made on the 30th of April 1768, a date when,
according to Washington's diary, he was at Eltham, Col. Bassett's plantation in New Kent County. According to his diary, Washington did
not arrive in Williamsburg until May 2. It is possible, but not probable,
that Lee saw Patcy at Eltham. More likely, the date in Washington's
ledger was not the date of payment, and that Lee saw Patcy on the
2nd or 3rd of May in Williamsburg.

2   John Mercer to George Mercer, December 22, 1767–January 28, 1768,
George Mercer Papers Relating to the Ohio Company of Virginia, Lois
Mulkearn, ed. (Pittsburgh, Pa, 1954) p. 204.

3   A Sephardic Jew, Dr. John De Sequeyra (1712–1795) resided in the
center section of what is now Shields Tavern on the south side of
Duke of Gloucester Street, near Capitol Square. Dr. William Pasteur,
who has been described as one of the first apothecaries in America and
who received his training at St. Thomas's Hospital in London, would
later take up residence in the William Finnie house on Francis Street
near the entrance to what is now Bassett Hall.

4   See *George Washington's Rules of Civility & Decent Behavior, in Company
and Conversation*, (Applewood Books, Bedford, Mass 1988).

5   Arthur Lee to George Washington, June 15, 1777, Donald Jackson ed.
and Dorothy Twohig, eds., *The Papers of George Washington, Revolution-*

ary War Series, (1775–1783), (12 vols., Charlottesville, VA, 1985–) 10: 43–44, (hereafter *"Papers, Revolutionary War Series"*); Donald Jackson, and Dorothy Twohig, eds. *The Papers of George Washington, The Diaries of George Washington,* (6 vols., Charlottesville, VA 1976–79), 2:74–75 (hereafter *"Diaries"*).

6   Edmund Randolph, *History of Virginia* (Charlottesville, VA 1970), p. 166; Gordon S. Wood, *The Creation of the American Republic 1776–1787* (Chapel Hill, NC 1969), p. 4; quoted in James Thomas Flexner, *George Washington* (4 vols., Boston MA, 1965–1972), 2:13.

7   Joseph J. Ellis, *His Excellency, George Washington* (New York, 2004), pp. xi–xii.

8   George Weedon to Nathaniel Greene, 5 Sep. 1781, *The Spirit of '76, The Story of the American Revolution as Told by Participants,* Henry Steele Commager and Richard B. Morris, eds., (1958; Da Capo Press, 1995), p. 1219.

9   "Lady Henrietta Liston's Journal of Washington's 'Resignation,' Retirement and Death," James C. Nicholls, ed., *Pennsylvania Magazine of History and Biography,* (1971) 95:511–520.

10 Nathaniel Wraxall, *The Historical and Posthumous Memoirs of Sir Nathaniel Wraxall,* 1772–1784, Henry B. Wheatley, ed. (5 vols; New York, 1884), 2: 137–142.

11 See Thomas Fleming, "The Man Who Would Not Be King," *MHQ: The Quarterly Journal of Military History* (Winter 1998), 10:2. (Casting doubt on whether this conversation ever took place.)

12 George Washington to Maj. Gen. Robert Howe, 22 Jan. 1781, John C. FitzPatrick, ed. *The Writings of George Washington from the Original Manuscript Sources, 1745–1799,* 39 vols; Charlottesville, VA 1931–1944), (hereafter, *Writings*) (21:128. "The object . . . is to compel the mutineers to unconditional submission, and I am to desire you will grant no terms while they are with arms in their hands in a state of resistance. The manner of executing this I leave to your discretion according to circumstances. If you succeed in compelling the revolted troops to surrender you will instantly execute a few of the most active and incendiary leaders."

13 George Washington to Lt. Col. John Laurens, April 9, 1781, *Writings,* 21: 436–440, 438, 439; *Diaries,* 2: 207–208.

14 *Diaries*, 3: 356–357; George Washington to the Marquis de Lafayette, 30 Jun., 1787I, *Writings*, 23:431–432.

15 *Diaries*, 2:207–09.

16 *Ibid.* His Virginia neighbors apparently agreed with this assessment. The seven members of the Virginia House of Delegates captured by Col. Banastre Tarleton in June of 1781 at Charlottesville told him frankly that "if England could prevent the intended cooperation of the French fleet and army with the American forces during the ensuing autumn, both Congress and the country would gladly dissolve the French alliance and enter into treaty with Great Britain." Tarleton passed the word to Cornwallis who passed it on to both the Ministry and Rear Adm. Sir Thomas Graves. Banastre Tarleton, *A History of the Campaigns of 1780 and 1781 in the Southern Provinces of North America*, (London, 1787), pp. 296–297.

17 Quoted in Flexner, *George Washington*, 2: 366–367.

18 George Washington to the Marquis de Lafayette, 14 Dec. 1780, *Writings*, 7: 322.

19 Willard Sterne Randall, "Why Benedict Arnold Did It," *American Heritage*, (Sept.–Oct. 1990), 41:60–73.

20 Quoted in Flexner, *George Washington*, 2: 430.

21 *Diaries*, 3:369.

22 *Ibid.*

23 *Diaries*, 3:370.

24 George Washington to the Comte de Rochambeau, 4 Jun. 1781, *Writings*, 22:157; see also, *Diaries*, 3:377.

25 George Washington to Chevalier de Chastellux, 13 Jun. 1781, *Writings*, 22:204–205.

26 George Washington to the Marquis de Lafayette, 21 May 1781, *Writings*, 22:143.

27 Flexner, *George Washington*, 2: 431.

28 See, Henry Clinton, *The American Rebellion: Sir Henry Clinton's Narrative of His Campaigns, 1775–1782, with an Appendix of Original Documents*, William B. Willcox, ed. (New Haven, CT, 1954), pp. 305–306. (Hereafter "Clinton, *The American Rebellion*")

29 For the argument supporting an intentional leaking, see Flexner, *George Washington in the American Revolution*, pp. 430–431.

30 George Washington to Noah Webster, 31 Jul. 1788, *Writings*, 9:402–404.

31 For the original French text of this dispatch, see Henri Doniol, *Histoire de la Participation de la France a l'Etablissement des Etats-Unis D'Amerique*, (5 tomes; Paris, 1892), 5:487–489.

32 Quoted in Flexner, *George Washington*, 2: 429–430.

33 George Washington to the Marquis de Lafayette, 30 Sep. 1779, *Memoirs, Correspondence and Manuscripts of General Lafayette*, (2 vols.; New York and London, 1838), 1: 307.

34 *Diaries*, 3: 378–384 n. 2.

35 "Journal of Jean-Francois-Louis, Comte de Clermonte-Crevecoeur," *The American Campaigns of Rochambeau's Army, 1780, 1781, 1782, 1783*, Howard C. Rice Jr., and Anne S. K. Brown, trans. and eds. (Princeton, 1972), p. 33. (hereafter "Journal of Clermonte-Crevecoeur"). For the most neatly dressed regiment (and best under fire), see von Closen's description of the mostly black Rhode Island Regiment in Closen, Baron Ludwig von. *The Revolutionary Journal of Baron Ludwig von Closen, 1780–1783*. Evelyn M. Acomb, trans. and ed. (Chapel Hill, N.C., 1958), (hereafter "Journal of von Closen"), p. 102.

36 *Diaries*, 3: 397.

37 *Ibid.*

38 Rochambeau, Marshal Count de, *Memoirs . . . relative to the War of Independence* (Paris, 1838), p. 44.

39 "Journal of von Closen," pp. 91–92.

40 *Ibid.*

41 *Diaries*, 3: 403–405.

42 *Diaries*, 3: 409–410.

43 *Diaries*, 3: 411–416.

44 George Washington to the Committee of Conference, 21 Aug. 1781, *Writings*, 23:30.

45 *Diaries*, 3: 416.

46 See *Diaries* 2:258; Henry P. Johnston, *The Yorktown Campaign*, (Philadelphia, PA, 1981), p. 92, (quoting from the diary of Robert Morris, American Superintendent of Finance); "Journal of Clermont-Crevecouer," pp. 46 and n.72

47 George Washington to the Marquis de Lafayette, 2 Sept. 1781, *Writ-*

ings, 23: 75–77.

48 Clinton, *The American Rebellion*, p. 563. "By intelligence which I have this day received, it would seem that Mr. Washington is moving an army to the southward with an appearance of haste, and gives out that he expects the cooperation of a considerable French armament. Your Lordship, however, may be assured that, if this should be the case, I shall either endeavour to reinforce the army under your command by all means within the compass of my power, or make every possible diversion in Your Lordship's favour."

49 *Diaries*, 3: 417. Not until later would Washington learn that de Grasse had been shadowed on his voyage up from the Caribbean by British Adm. Sir Samuel Hood and his fleet of 14 ships of the line. Thinking that de Grasse was headed north, Hood sailed on to New York, where he united his fleet with that of British naval commander Adm. Graves. Only then did the two admirals realize that the target was Virginia. At once, Graves sailed for the mouth of the Chesapeake with a combined fleet of 20 ships. There, on the 5th of September, he gave battle to de Grasse's 24 ships of the line. Thanks to a lack of coordination between the signalizing systems used on Hood's and Grave's ships, only the British van was able to engage with the French fleet, the seven ships in the British rear under Hood never getting within range of the French. Three of Graves' ships were badly damaged, but he pursued de Grasse's fleet until it gave him the slip, then sailed back to the Bay where he found Adm. de Barras and the French fleet from Newport. With only 18 ships fit for battle against a combined French fleet of 36 ships of the line, Graves had no choice but to return to New York.

50 Quoted in Flexner, *George Washington*, 2: 443. Maximilian Joseph, the Compte de Deux Ponts (called "Zweibrücken"), was a member of a branch of the ruling family of Bavaria, the Wittelsbachs. In the final days of the war, he was captured by a young British Captain, Horatio Nelson, who entertained Zweibrücken for a few days and then let him go. He later became Elector of Bavaria in 1799 only to be promoted to King by Napoleon in 1805.

51 *Ibid.*

52 James Thacher, M.D., *Military Journal of the American Revolution, 1775–1783*, (1862; Gansevoort, N.Y., 1998), p. 269.

53 *Ibid.*, pp. 271–272.

54 *Ibid.*, p. 272.

55 General Orders, 6 Sep. 1781, *Writings*, 23:93–94.

56 Quoted in Flexner, *George Washington*, 2: 443–444.

57 *The Trumbull Papers*, Collections of the Mass. Hist. Soc., 7th Series (6 vols.; Boston, 1902), 1: 333.

58 George Washington to Gen. Benjamin Lincoln, 15 Sep. 1781, *Writings*, 23: 119.

59 George Washington to the Marquis de Lafayette, 10 Sep. 1781, *Writings*, 23: 110.

60 There are no entries in Washington's diary from September 10 to 16, for the perhaps obvious reason that with victory in sight, he had no need or time for a diary. Nor was he likely to stop to register the changes he saw in Williamsburg, a town that had been the center of his hopes for 28 years – from his courting of Martha at the Custis mansion on Francis Street, to his dinners at Speaker Randolph's house on Market Square to his boys' nights out at the theater with Lord Dunmore. Williamsburg was no longer the capital of Virginia. Jefferson had had it moved to Richmond in 1780, ostensibly to protect it from British. Despite that, Williamsburg was still (according to one observer) "a handsome" town, with "two handsome edifices," the College and the Capitol building, at either end of Gloucester Street. The "handsomeness" of the College was mostly a façade. Another observer, someone who took the trouble to actually enter the College, found it being used as a military hospital; in addition to the usual horrors it was daubed with feces. The Palace too was "in very bad condition," though it was evident that "Lord Dunmore had once lived there in great style. "Journal" of von Closen," pp. 165–166.

61 Col. St. George Tucker to Francis Tucker, 15 Sep. 1781, quoted in Mary Haldane Coleman, *St. George Tucker, Citizen of No Mean City*, (Richmond, 1938), pp. 70–71.

62 *Ibid.*

63 Max Farrand, ed., *The Records of the Federal Convention of 1787*, (3 vols., New Haven, 1911), 3: 85–86.

64 St. George Tucker to Francis Tucker, 15 Sep. 1781, quoted in Coleman, *St. George Tucker*, p. 70.

65 "Col. Richard Butler's Journal," *Yorktown, Climax of the Revolution*, (Nat. Park Serv. Sourcebook, Series Number One: Yorktown, 1941), www.nps.gov/history/history/online_books/source/sb1/sb1toc.htm (accessed 11/11/2011).

66 St. George Tucker to Francis Tucker, 15 Sep. 1781, quoted in Coleman, *St. George Tucker*, p. 70.

67 See "Col. Richard Butler's Journal," www.nps.gov/history/history/online_books/source/sb1/sb1toc.htm (accessed 11/11/2011)

68 "Military Journal of Major Ebenezer Denny," in *We Were There, Descriptions of Williamsburg, 1699–1859*, Jane Carson, ed., (Williamsburg and Charlottesville, 1965), pp. 53–54.

69 Quoted in Flexner, *George Washington*, 2: 449. This whole story is a bit too much for Flexner, who doubts whether the "fat stomach" of Gen. Knox, the American artillery commander, could have "rocked . . . with laughter" or whether Washington, tasked with "represent[ing] the dignity of the United States" was likely to have been amused. I say, "Why not?" This was a meeting between two allies who had every reason to believe that they were on the verge of an epochal victory. Why should they not enjoy themselves – before everyone got down to business. More to the point, the failure to allow Washington his humanity in instances like this, even at some cost to his dignity, is one of the reasons that he remains so remote.

70 *Diaries*, 3: 136..

71 George Washington to Adm. de Grasse, 25 Sep.1781, *Writings*, 23: 136–139.

72 Silenced, but not done. As Flexner notes, after de Grasse had "calmed down" he sent Washington a testy letter reminding him that he had "more at heart" in a favorable outcome to the campaign than Washington himself. Flexner, *George Washington*, 2: 451.

73 "Journal of Clermont-Crevecoeur," p. 57.

74 Joseph Plumb Martin, *Private Yankee Doodle*, George E. Scheer, ed., (1962; Philadelphia, PA, 1998), p. 228.

75 "Journal of Clermont-Crevecoeur," p. 57.

76 "Journal of Colonel Jonathan Trumbull, Secretary to George Washington," in *The Spirit of Seventy-Six*, pp. 1227–1228.

77 *Ibid.*, p. 1228.

78 "Diary of James Duncan," in *The Spirit of Seventy Six*, pp. 1228–1229.

79 "Col. Richard Butler's Journal," www.nps.gov/history/history/online_books/source/sb1/sb1toc.htm (accessed 11/11/2011). Washington also wielded the first pickaxe in the building of the first parallel.

80 Thacher, *Military Journal*, p. 284.

81 Martin, *Private Yankee Doodle*, p. 233.

82 "Ebenezer Denny, Journal, September 1 – November 1 1781," in *The American Revolution, Writings from the War of Independence*, John Rhodehamel, ed. (New York, 2001), p. 723.

83 Thacher, *Military Journal*, p. 283.

84 "St. George Tucker: Journal, September 28 – October 20, 1781," in *The American Revolution, Writings from the War of Independence*, p. 727.

85 *Ibid.*, p. 734.

86 "Journal of Jean-Baptiste Antoine de Verger," *The American Campaigns of Rochambeau's Army, 1780, 1781,1782, 1783*, Howard C. Rice, Jr., and Anne S. K. Brown, trans and eds., (Princeton, NJ, 1972), p. 142.

87 *Ibid.*

88 Martin, *Private Yankee Doodle*, pp.235–236.

89 *Ibid.*, p. 236.

90 Thacher, *Military Journal*, pp. 285–286 fn.

91 *Ibid.*, pp. 285–286.

92 *Ibid.*, pp. 286–287.

93 *Ibid.*, pp. 288–289.

94 *Ibid.*, p. 289. "The World Turned Upside Down" is little more than a catalogue of improbable events:

> If buttercups buzzed after the bee,
> If boats were on land, churches on sea,
> If ponies rode men and grass ate the cows,
> And cats should be chased to holes by the mouse,
> If the mamas sold their babies to the gypsies for half a crown;
> Summer were spring and the t'other side round,
> Then all the world would be upside down.

95 *Ibid.*

96 *Ibid.*

97 *Ibid.*, pp. 289–290. One New Jersey officer spoke of how the "British officers in general behaved like little boys who had been whipped at school. Some bit their lips; some pouted; others cried." Quoted in *The Spirit of Seventy-Six*, p. 1239.

98 *Ibid.*

99 Gen. Cornwallis to Sir Henry Clinton, 20 Oct., 1781, "Cornwallis Surrenders, Virginia, October, 1781," *The American Revolution, Writings from the War of Independence*, pp.744–749.

100 "Lord North: 'Oh God! It Is All Over,'" *The American Revolution, Writings from the War of Independence*, pp. 1243–1245.

101 *Ibid.*, p. 1245.

102 Thacher, *Military Journal*, p. 285.

103 Ellis, *His Excellency*, pp. 141–146, 141.

104 *Writings*, 10: 170.

105 John Frederick Shroeder and Edward C. Towne, *Life and Times of Washington*, (2 vols.; 1903; Kessinger Pub. Co., 2005), 2: 1491.

106 "Washington Resigns his Commission: Annapolis, December 1783," *The American Revolution, Writings from the War of Independence*, pp. 793–795, 794.

107 Richard Brookhiser, *Founding Father: Rediscovering George Washington* (New York, 1996), p. 4.

108 Gouverneur Morris, *An Oration Upon the Death of General Washington*, (New York, 1800), p. 4.

109 Quoted in Ellis, *His Excellency*, p. 149. (Ellis' evaluation of Washington's state of mind is well worth reading.)

110 *Virginia Gazette* (Rind), 14 Apr. 1768. The *Beggar's Opera* was scheduled to open on June 3.

111 Paul K. Longmore, *The Invention of George Washington*, (Charlottesville, VA 1999), p. 219.

112 Carl J. Richard, *The Founders and the Classics, Greece, Rome and the American Enlightenment*, (Cambridge, 1994), p. 58.

113 *Ibid.*, p. 60.

114 Joseph Addison, *Cato: A Tragedy and Selected Essays*, Christine Dunn Henderson and Mark E. Yellin, eds. (Indianapolis, IN 2004), p. 44.

115 George Washington to Sarah Cary Fairfax, 12 Sept., 1758, *Papers,*

Colonial Series, 6: 10–13 and George Washington to Sarah Cary Fairfax, 25 Sept., 1758, *ibid*, 6: 41–43.

116 Ellis, *His Excellency*, p. 36; Don Higginbotham, *Revolution In America, Considerations & Comparisons*, (Charlottesville, 2005), p. 63; Longmore, *The Invention of George Washington*, pp. 182–183 and n. 34. While it is true, as Don Higginbotham notes in *Revolution in America*, that the "weight of scholarly opinion now holds that Washington had fallen in love with his friend's wife," speculation as to the exact nature of the relationship remains fierce.

117 Addison, *Cato*, p. 11. Zama, the capital of Numidia, is in present day Tunisia.

118 Addison, *Cato*, p. 78.

119 Ellis, *His Excellency*, p. 37.

120 Addison, *Cato*, pp. 96, 81, 84; Longmore, *The Invention of George Washington*, p. 17; Addison, *Cato*, p. 84 (spoken by Juba).

121 Addison, *Cato*, pp. 96, 44.

122 *George Washington's Rules of Civility*, p. 12.

123 George Washington to Sally C. Fairfax, 21 May, 1798, W.W. Abbott ed., *The Papers of George Washington: The Retirement Series*, (4 vols., Charlottesville, VA, 1998–1999), 2:272–73 (hereafter "*Papers, Retirement Series*"). Among the important events Washington was alluding to were his appointment as commander in chief of the American Army, winning the Revolutionary War, presiding at the Constitutional Convention, his election as the first President of the United States (and reelection to that office), followed by his retirement to Mount Vernon and formal assumption of the role of "Father Of His Country."

124 George Washington to Sarah Cary Fairfax, 25 Sept., 1758, *Papers, Colonial Series*, 6: 41–43.

125 Arthur Lee, "Monitor I," *The Farmer's and Monitor's Letters to the Inhabitants of the British Colonies*, (William Rind, Williamsburg, VA, 1769; Virginia Independence Bicentennial Edition, 1969), p. 61.

126 Thomas Jefferson to Dr. Walter Jones, 2 Jan., 1814, *Jefferson's Writings*, Lipscomb and Bergh, eds., (20 vols.; Washington D.C., 1903–1907) 14:49; Abigail Adams to John Adams, 16 Jul. 16, 1775, [electronic edition]. *Adams Family Papers: An Electronic Archive*. Massachusetts Historical Society. http://www.masshist.org/digitaladams/. (accessed

10/27/2011.)

127 Longmore, *The Invention of George Washington*, p.173.

128 John H.Gwathmey, *The Historical Register of Virginians in the Revolution*, (1938; Genealogical Publishing Co., 1973), pp. 490, 288

129 "Muster Roll for Oct. 1777," 14th Regiment, 1777–78 (Folder 327) [NARA Roll 112], National Archives And Records Administration, U.S. Revolutionary War Rolls, 1775–1783 (Microfilm).

130 Gwathmey, *Register*, p. 288.

131 Samuel M. Wilson, *Catalogue of Revolutionary Soldiers and Sailors of the Commonwealth of Virginia to Whom Land Bounty Rights Were Granted by Virginia for Military Services in the War for Independence*, (1913; Heritage Books, 2006), p. 28.

132 Malcolm Hart Harris, M.D., *Old New Kent County [Virginia]: Some Accounts of the Planters, Plantations and Places in New Kent County*, (1977; Genealogical Pub. Co., Baltimore MD, 2006), pp. 683–684.

Acknowledgements

Dr. Samuel Johnson once said, "It is wonderful how a man will sometimes turn over half a library to make just one book." After ten years of nearly constant work on this series, I find that I have not only turned over half a library, but a good part of my life. New friends have become old ones. Some very good friends who read the essays in this series in their very earliest versions are now gone. Meanwhile, the library – I am speaking of the ever-expanding library of the internet – has only gotten larger.

It is impossible to name everyone who helped make this series, but some I must mention. There would be no series without the love, encouragement and help of my wife, Joan Morrow. But for the welcoming attitude, expert assistance and criticism of two truly fine historians of the period, Rhys Isaac and James Horn, I would still be trying to distinguish the forest from the trees. The encouragement I received from my two chief non professional readers, Joan and Terry Thomas, turned a mere collection of dates, people and events into a study of the character of Williamsburg. Other people who read one or more of the essays and made helpful comments include my 90-year-old aunt Rosemary Bauder, Paul and Joan Wernick, Richard Schumann, Bill Barker, Michael Fincham, Ken and Judith Simmons, Fred Fey, Cary Carson, Jon Kite, Al Louer, Bob Hill and Collen Isaac. I also wish in particular to thank Jon Kite for obtaining the French army dossier of John Skey Eustace and for translating one of Jack Eustace's overwrought pamphlets from the French. Richard Schumann, James Horn and Roger Hudson kindly consented to do prefaces for one of the booklets in this series. Al Louer and Paul Freiling of Colonial Williamsburg arranged for me to see Williamsburg from the roof of the Governor's Palace, a view that put time itself in perspective .

Those who are subscribers to the British quarterly, *Slightly Foxed*, described on its website as "The Real Reader's Quarterly," will recognize some similarities between the booklets in this series and that magazine. The resemblance is no accident. When I saw *Slightly Foxed* for the first time, I immediately realized that it was the perfect model, in size, material and design for what I was looking for. With that in mind, I contacted Andrew Evans at 875 Design, the English book design firm responsible for its appearance, and asked him if would be willing to take on this project. He said, "yes," and it was not long before he and I had assembled a team of people who not only seemed to know what I wanted but were able to give me something I never expected to find: new ideas on the subject matter. I especially want to thank Gail Pirkis, the publisher of *Slightly Foxed*, for recommending Roger Hudson as editor for this series. Roger is not only a highly accomplished writer in his own right, he is truly a writer's editor.

Sadly, the genial spirit who presided over the series, read and commented on virtually every booklet and guided me through its development, died while the series was still in production. I am speaking of Rhys Isaac, the Pulitzer Prize-winning author of what is still the best book ever written on late colonial Virginia, *The Transformation of Virginia*. Rhys' presence at our dinner table will be deeply missed. But he will also be missed from the profession of history, where his exuberant writing style and elegiac approach to the past daily gave the lie to the sour souls who think history is about settling scores.

As I began these Acknowledgments with a quotation from

Samuel Johnson I would like to end with one *about* Johnson. It was spoken by someone who did not know him well, but knew of him very well, William Gerard Hamilton. For me, it is Rhys Isaac's epitaph: " He has made a chasm, which not only nothing can fill up, but which nothing has a tendency to fill up. – Johnson is dead. – Let us go to the next best; – There is no nobody; – no man can be said to put you in mind of Johnson."

WILLIAMSBURG IN CHARACTER

About the Author

GEORGE MORROW brings a lifetime of experience to bear on the characters of the people featured in this series. He has been a university instructor, lawyer, general counsel for a *Fortune* 100 company, the CEO of two major health care organizations and a management consultant. He received his academic training in textual analysis and literary theory from Rutgers and Brown Universities. He lives in Williamsburg with his wife, Joan, and two in-your-face Siamese cats, Pete and Pris.

Other Books by George T. Morrow II in the
WILLIAMSBURG IN CHARACTER SERIES

A Cock and Bull for Kitty
Lord Dunmore and the Affair that Ruined
the British Cause in Virginia

The Greatest Lawyer that Ever Lived
Patrick Henry at the Bar of History

The Day They Buried Great Britain
Francis Fauquier, Lord Botetourt and The Fate of Nations

Williamsburg at Dawn
The Duel That Touched Off A Revolution In Arthur Lee

Of Heretics, Traitors and True Believers
The War for the Soul of Williamsburg

Forthcoming
Patrick Henry to Lord Dunmore
"We Must Fight!"

WILLIAMSBURG IN CHARACTER